Annie Oakley in England, 1887. (Photo by Elliott & Fry, London)

ANNIE OAKLEY
AND BUFFALO BILL'S WILD WEST

Isabelle S. Sayers

Dover Publications, Inc.
New York

Picture Credits

Author and publisher are grateful to the following suppliers of pictures
for the present volume.

Rush Blakeley Collection (Greenville, Ohio): Figs. 55, 84.

Buffalo Bill Historical Center (Cody, Wyoming): Figs. 22, 24, 36, 41, 43, 45, 51, 66, 67, 74.

Cincinnati (Ohio) Historical Society: Fig. 9.

Circus World Museum (Baraboo, Wisconsin): Figs. 15, 63, 65, 79, 80, 82, 91.

Albert Conover Collection (Xenia, Ohio): Figs. 8, 14, 16.

Denver (Colorado) Public Library, Western History Department: Frontispiece, Figs. 20, 21, 26, 27, 31, 33, 44, 49, 50, 52, 53, 54, 57, 61, 64, 69, 71, 73, 75, 76, 77, 78, 83.

Stella Foote Collection: Figs. 18, 19, 25, 32, 34, 37, 46 (taken from the originals in the "Treasures of the West" collection and reproduced in *Letters from Buffalo Bill* by Stella Foote).

Garst Museum (Greenville, Ohio): Figs. 1, 3, 6, 7, 23, 38, 56, 60, 86, 87, 90, 92, 94, 95, 96, 99.

Gordon D. Hoffman Collection (Green Lake, Wisconsin): Fig. 88.

Ithaca Gun Company (Ithaca, New York): Fig. 93.

Library of Congress, Prints & Photographs Division (Washington, D.C.): Figs. 30, 35.

National Archives (Washington, D.C.): Fig. 58 (U.S. Signal Corps, photo number 111-SC-85680).

Nebraska State Historical Society (Lincoln): Fig. 70.

Notman Photographic Archives, McCord Museum, McGill University (Montreal): Figs. 13, 28, 29.

Ohio Historical Society (Columbus): Figs. 2, 5, 10, 11.

Remington Gun Museum (Ilion, New York): Fig. 85.

Ringling Museum of the Circus (Sarasota, Florida): Figs. 42, 48.

Western History Collections, University of Oklahoma (Norman): Figs. 39, 40, 47.

Miriam Wilson Collection (Dayton, Ohio): Fig. 12.

Illustrations not credited are from the author's collection (photocopies by John Dobos and Rittenhouse).

Published in Canada by General Publishing Company, Ltd., 30 Lesmill Road, Don Mills, Toronto, Ontario.
Published in the United Kingdom by Constable and Company, Ltd., 10 Orange Street, London WC2H 7EG.

Annie Oakley and Buffalo Bill's Wild West is a new work, first published by Dover Publications, Inc., in 1981.

International Standard Book Number: 0-486-24120-3
Library of Congress Catalog Card Number: 80-69158

Manufactured in the United States of America
Dover Publications, Inc.
180 Varick Street
New York, N.Y. 10014

Foreword

Annie Oakley's life paralleled the rise and fall of Wild West shows and she is undoubtedly one of the best-known exponents of this bygone entertainment. Her skill developed during a time when women weren't even allowed to vote, yet she excelled in a man's sport and never lost her feminine appeal.

As a performer, she spanned half a century, starting with neighborhood turkey shoots, then touring the vaudeville circuits and later joining the Sells Brothers Circus. However, she achieved her greatest fame during her 17 years with William F. Cody's unequaled Buffalo Bill's Wild West. During one summer of discontent, Annie joined Gordon W. Lillie's Pawnee Bill Historical Wild West Exhibition, but later went back with Cody.

Later, after years of public shooting exhibitions, Annie joined a small Wild West group headed by Vernon Seavers. Her last public appearance was at Vandalia, Ohio, the summer before she died.

Annie Oakley's talent was recognized by the thousands of people who saw her perform in the United States, Canada and Europe during her long career. Today her name is included in the dictionary as slang, denoting a pass or free ticket. Free passes are always punched so they can be identified and not counted in the cash tally. Annie often shot holes in small cards during a performance and the resemblance was noticed—hence the slang expression.

Her life and legends have been pictured in movies, on stage and TV and in books. She was best known as a disciplined performer, but to close friends, she was loved as a gentle, generous woman—truly a beautiful person.

The illustrations in this book represent some of the facets of the incredible life of Annie Oakley.

Contents

1

Girlhood

No more unlikely a background for an internationally known markswoman could be imagined than that of Annie Oakley! Her parents, Jacob and Susan Moses, were Quakers who reared their children in a quiet, religious manner. Yet from this modest environment emerged one of the world's most famous entertainers.

Family tradition tells how a mature Jacob fell in love with 15-year-old Susan Wise and, after obtaining permission from her parents, placed her on a pillion and took her away on his horse. After their marriage in Blair County, Pennsylvania, in 1850, they became the parents of Mary Jane, Lyda and Elizabeth.

The Moseses kept a small inn near the termination of the eastern division of the Pennsylvania Canal at Hollidaysburg. One night, after a careless guest upset an oil lamp, the log tavern burned to the ground and the family was homeless. The year was 1855. Jacob had heard so much about the fertile Ohio country that he decided to pack up what few possessions they had left and to move West. The Quakers allowed their members to carry a gun as a necessary tool of survival on the frontier, and we know Jacob took his muzzle-loader with him. It was this very gun that later launched one of his daughters into a phenomenal career.

Mr. and Mrs. Moses settled on a small rented farm in northern Darke County, Ohio, and five more children were born. After Sarah Ellen came Phoebe Ann (Annie) on August 13, 1860, and later John and Hulda. One daughter died in infancy.

Jacob died of pneumonia on February 11, 1866, leaving Susan with little but their lively family of seven. She tried to keep her home together by going into the community as a practical nurse, but jobs were scarce and the pay small.

When the widow Moses married Dan Brumbaugh, it looked as if the family fortunes were greatly improved—but not for long. He died after an accident and she again had to assume the responsibility of supporting her growing family. At his death, their daughter Emily was only five months old.

Mrs. Crawford Edington, matron at the Darke County Infirmary, offered to take Annie and train her in exchange for help with the children. In a Darke County history, George W. Wolfe describes what must have been a deplorable condition at the home:

> Many persons incapable of attending to their own wants were housed at the Infirmary and a shortage of rooms compelled the children to associate with these unfortunates, whose habits of life and language were not intended to exert that influence for good that should always surround the child.

Apparently, the Infirmary was the dumping ground for the elderly, the orphaned and the insane. Perhaps this early experience, working at such a place, aroused in Annie the tremendous compassion she had for children wherever she went.

Mrs. Edington taught her a skill and appreciation for fine sewing which helped when she later made her own costumes. It must be pointed out that the Edingtons tried to make life tolerable for the inmates with all the resources they could find. Later, a larger home was built and the children were separated from the adults.

1. *Annie Oakley's mother, née Susan Wise. (Photo by C. M. Hengen, Versailles, Ohio)*

2. *The Darke County Infirmary in 1870. 3. Annie's stepfather Joseph Shaw. 4. The Shaw cabin near North Star, Ohio. 5. Annie as a purveyor of game.*

5

Many years after Annie lived with the Edingtons, their son Frank related:

Mother couldn't stand to see her placed with the other children and brought her over to our living quarters in another part of the institution. We went to school together. After she left and became famous, Mother and she kept up a correspondence that continued until Mother's death.

I can't think her skill with firearms was the most important factor in causing the people of the world to hold her in such esteem. It was the fine unexplainable personality that gripped and held them.

When Annie was given an opportunity to work as a mother's helper in a private home south of Greenville, she discovered much more was expected of her than she could possibly endure. She was lonesome and frightened and unable to communicate with her mother, who lived north of town.

Finally, in desperation, Annie ran away from her employer and tried to locate her mother. She discovered that in her absence, Joseph Shaw had become her new stepfather and had built a cabin for his wife and children near North Star. At last Susan had a permanent home—complete with orchard, garden and cellar—where she planted, harvested and stored the surplus for winter.

Like all pioneer children, the Moses brood was expected to do their share of farm chores before play. Since the three oldest Moses daughters were married and gone, Annie, being the eldest girl at home, assumed many household tasks. Though she loved her sister Hulda and half-sister Emily Brumbaugh, she spent most of her free time with her only brother, John.

John, who was two years younger, helped his sister when she first used their father's old gun to down an unwary rabbit. In an interview in 1914, Annie said:

When I first commenced shooting in the field of Ohio, my gun was a single-barrel muzzle-loader and, as well as I can remember, was 16-bore. I used black powder, cut my own wads out of cardboard boxes, and thought I had the best gun on earth. Anyway, I managed to kill a great many ruffed grouse, quail and rabbits, all of which were quite plentiful in those days.

My father [probably her stepfather, Joseph Shaw] was a mail carrier and made two trips a week to Greenville, which was the county seat, a distance of 20 or 40 miles a day—not very far in these days of good roads. On each trip he carried my game, which he exchanged for ammunition, groceries and necessities. A few years ago, I gave an exhibition at Greenville, and met the old gentleman who had bought all of my game. He showed me some old account books showing the amount of game he had purchased. I won't say how much, as I might be classed as a game-hog, but any man who has ever tried to make a living and raise a family on 27 acres of poor land will readily understand that it was a hard proposition, and that every penny derived from the sale of game shipped helped.

The great performer Fred Stone, a friend in later years, reported she once told him: "From the time I was nine, I never had a nickel I did not earn for myself."

The storekeeper mentioned in the quotation was Charles Katzenberger, who bought Annie's game and shipped it to hotels in Cincinnati and Dayton and to the famous Golden Lamb in Lebanon. The diners at Bevis House in Cincinnati often commented to the manager, Jack Frost, how much they appreciated not finding shot in their game dinners. Annie was so good, she shot each critter in the head.

The modest Shaw cabin was home to Annie for several more years, and it was here she returned between show tours in her later life. She delighted in sending money to her mother to buy new berry bushes or an especially fine fruit tree, because she knew how much pleasure her mother took in "putting up" fruit for the winter.

2
Marriage and Early Career

When Jack Frost, the Cincinnati hotelkeeper who bought some of Annie's game, discovered she was visiting her sister, Mrs. Joseph Stein, in town, he decided to match the youthful huntress with a professional sharpshooter. A trio of marksmen headed by Frank Butler was appearing at a local theater, and Frost thought this competition would be a great Thanksgiving afternoon entertainment. Butler agreed to the contest but was dumbfounded when he discovered his opponent was a diminutive country girl.

"Kentucky Frank," who later ran a shooting gallery on North Vine Street in Cincinnati, told a reporter about witnessing the famous match between Annie Moses and Butler. Butler killed his first bird. Annie stepped to the post and when she called, "Pull," got a dark, lively pigeon, which she managed to shoot. They were tied until Butler missed a fast, quavering bird. Annie was ahead until she too had a miss, leaving them tied. The last bird was a hard one and Butler missed. She killed her twenty-fifth bird and won the match. This was quite a feat for a girl who had never shot trap-released birds before. As far as can be determined, the match was held in 1875. The area in which it was held, northeast of Cincinnati near the route of the Cincinnati Northern Railroad, was called Oakley.

Frank Butler was hardly what a Quaker mother would choose as an ideal mate for her shy daughter Ann, but nevertheless court her he did. Besides his vaudeville career, Mrs. Shaw might have objected to the fact that Frank was divorced and in debt when he and her daughter first met.

Frank was a sentimental Irishman who had emigrated to the States when just a boy. Unskilled but determined, he managed to support himself with a variety of jobs. First he delivered milk with a pony cart in New York City, next he was a stable boy and later became a fisherman.

Mrs. Shaw liked Frank and, after gaining her consent, Annie and Frank were married in 1876, thus beginning a happy 50 years together. During the first years, while Frank was on tour, Annie stayed with her mother and tried to improve her education, which had been inter-

6. *Annie Moses Butler, about 1880. (Photo by Martin, Chicago)*
7. *Frank Butler, about 1880. (Photo by Martin, Chicago)*

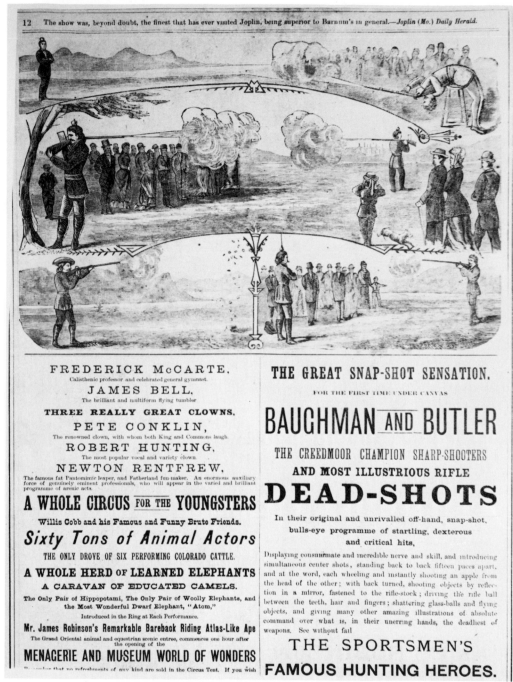

8. *The Baughman and Butler act, as advertised in the Sells Brothers Circus Courier, 1881.*

rupted as a child. In 1877 Frank became a naturalized American citizen.

Always patient with animals, Frank had started his stage career with a group of trained dogs, but eventually developed a shooting act that was booked into theaters. Frank later teamed up with a performer named Baughman and they were billed in the Sells Brothers Circus Courier for 1881 as "The Creedmoor Champion Sharp-Shooters and Most Illustrious Rifle Dead-Shots" and as "The Sportsmen's Famous Hunting Heroes."

A devoted husband wrote the following from Quincy, Illinois, on May 9, 1881:

LITTLE RAIN DROPS

There's a charming little girl
She's many miles from here.
She's a loving little fairy
You'd fall in love to see her.
Her presence would remind you
Of an angel in the skies,
And you bet I love this little girl
With the rain drops in her eyes.

Some fine day I'll settle down
And stop this roving life;
With a cottage in the country

9. *Strobridge Lithographic Co. poster for the Graham and Butler act, 1882.*

I will claim my little wife.
Then we will be happy and contented,
No quarrels shall arise
And I'll never leave my little girl
With the rain drops in her eyes.

Evidently, this tribute was sent with a gift, because Frank also wrote: "Now you can wear this to church Sunday, as I am going to send it now. Aren't you my little girl?"

John Graham was Frank's partner. On May 1, 1882, the act "Graham & Butler" was booked into Crystal Hall, Springfield, Ohio. When Graham became ill, Annie took his place in the act. Even though she was unaccustomed to appearing before an audience and shooting by artificial light, she was determined to do her best, and this she did. Courtney Ryley Cooper, in *Annie Oakley, Woman at Arms*, wrote about this occasion, the start of her long career, as follows:

That was an attribute of Annie Oakley that she took nothing into consideration save her determination to do the thing upon which she had set her mind. A strange combination of human nature, this little woman of Darke County beginnings. As mild as an April shower, apparently as unsophisticated as though she had come but yesterday

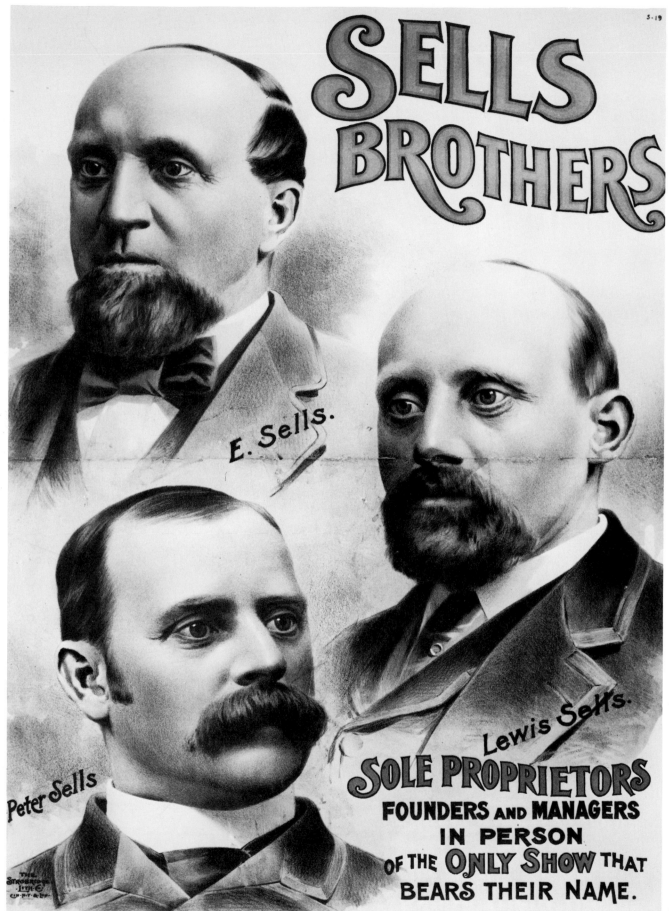

SELLS BROTHERS

E. Sells.

Lewis Sells.

Peter Sells

SOLE PROPRIETORS
FOUNDERS AND **MANAGERS**
IN PERSON
OF THE ONLY SHOW THAT
BEARS THEIR NAME.

10

10. *Strobridge poster for the Sells Brothers Circus.* 11. *The Sells Brothers show on a lot in the 1880s. A number of the ornate tableau wagons are aligned at the left.*

from the backwoods which produced her beginnings, kindly to a point that went far beyond the usual definitions of thoughtfulness, her nature contained also a quality that savored of the strength of steel. Perhaps it came from the exigencies of her youth, the trials, the sufferings; perhaps it was ingrained from a mother who had been forced to smile in the face of misfortune for the greater part of her life, but it was there; a sublime form of self-confidence, wholly without ego, which caused Annie Oakley, once she had considered a feat or a task, to believe wholly and utterly that she could perform it—and then go ahead and do that which she believed! It was with this attitude that she looked upon a future career as a stage shot, and she went to her first performance with the assurance of one who had been doing it always.

The *Springfield Daily Republic* makes no mention of Annie's first stage appearance, but it does mention that

an epidemic was rampant in Springfield at the time— smallpox! Persons dying in the night were buried before sunup. It is a wonder there were any public gatherings allowed.

When Annie joined her husband's act, she decided she needed a stage name, and since they had first met on the shooting grounds at Oakley, Ohio, this was what she chose. Today, a hundred years later, Oakley is part of greater Cincinnati.

She also decided she needed a costume that was more appropriate for the theater than street clothes. Being a practical person, she used durable material, but designed her costumes with such a flair they were often copied by couturiers during her later European tours. She ruled out the use of leather as being too hard to keep clean. She even fashioned her own leggings, which she wore with short skirts.

"Butler and Oakley" and their valuable acting dogs, Jack and George, often appeared as a "specialty." This was a rather brief entertainment that went on while the scenery was being shifted between acts of a play. Grad-

12

ually their fame as rifle experts spread, and their bookings weren't so chancy.

As part of their act, George, a standard-bred poodle, sat on a pedestal with an apple on his head and allowed his master to shatter it. At the end of the performance, he too would bow. An elderly George accompanied the Butlers during their first season with Buffalo Bill's Wild West in 1885. When the dog died in Cleveland, Ohio, his casket was fashioned by one of the Wild West carpenters, and he was wrapped in the elaborate pedestal cover that had been part of his act.

An unusual document included in the Annie Oakley files at the Garst Museum, Greenville, Ohio, is a copy of a marriage certificate indicating that Francis E. Butler and Annie Moses, both of Saginaw, Michigan, were united in the rite of holy matrimony by Thomas Manon, officiating minister, on June 20, 1882, in Windsor, Canada.

Frank Butler had been married previously and was the father of a son and a daughter, but was divorced when he first met Annie. Perhaps he later discovered his divorce was not final at the time of his marriage to the Ohio lass in 1876, and this necessitated another ceremony in 1882. By that time both of them were signed up with the Sells Brothers Circus.

The four Sells Brothers of Dublin, Ohio—Ephraim, Lewis, Allen and Peter—organized their first wagon circus in 1871 with one tent and a few sideshow features. By 1878 they had added more performers and tents and now traveled by rail (unfortunately, two wrecks marred that season, one in Pennsylvania and one in Ohio). In the early 1880s the circus was doing quite well.

Since the Butlers were now a team, it was natural that Annie wanted to travel with her husband during his engagement with Sells in 1883, but she appeared only as an equestrienne that first year. In the course of the season she led a sit-down strike against the Sells management when she felt a saddle was unsafe. She was told the saddle was all right, but she jerked the rotted girth and the saddle fell to the ground. It was show time and the opening feature, the "Rose Garland" executed by 12 riders, was omitted on this particular day. On another occasion, she protested against the living quarters contracted for by the management.

In the fall and winter 1883–1884 Annie and Frank toured with a three-act play, *Slocum's Oath*, a companion piece to Frank I. Frayne's *Si Slocum*. The publicity described the play as a "poetical sensation replete with thrilling situations and wonderful mechanical effects." The "Premier Shots," Butler and Oakley, were competing with the abilities of a trained bear named Jenny and the $2,000 acting dogs Jack and George.

While acting in St. Paul, the Butlers had a famous backstage visitor—Sitting Bull. He was tremendously impressed with Annie Oakley's performance and thought she was possessed of the Good Spirit—that no one could ever hurt her, that only those supernaturally blessed could have so sure an aim. When he was introduced to her, they exchanged pictures and he adopted her, giving

13. *Sitting Bull, 1885. (Photo by William Notman, Montreal)*

her the name "Watanya cicilia," translated as "Little Sure Shot."

Although still a political prisoner, Sitting Bull was permitted to leave the Standing Rock Agency at Fort Yates, Dakota Territory, on several occasions (permission first had to be granted by James McLaughlin, Indian agent at the fort). One of Sitting Bull's trips was to the St. Paul gala that marked the completion of the Northern Pacific Railway in 1883; this transcontinental line now linked Lake Superior with Puget Sound. It was probably during this trip that he first met Annie Oakley.

Kate E. Glaspell, in the *North Dakota Quarterly*, tells an interesting story about why the Indian leader was there:

> Probably the greatest celebration [of the railway] was the first, given in St. Paul. Many wealthy men of that city were interested in the venture and they thought it would be unique and interesting to have one of the welcoming speeches given by an Indian, so they asked a soldier, familiar with their language, to bring Sitting Bull, chief of the great Sioux tribe, down with him and to prepare a speech for his delivery, to be interpreted by the soldier

12. *Annie as an equestrienne for the Sells Brothers, 1883, wearing the habit in which she rode sidesaddle in the "Rose Garland" feature.*

A Correct Bird's Eye View Showing the Tents of the Great Show. Arrival of Excursion Trains, which bring thousands of people daily·to·see the Only·Big·50·Cage

14

14. *The expanded Sells Brothers Circus*. 15. *"Butler and Oakley" in Sells advertising, 1884.*

himself. Everything worked out well and they arrived prepared to make a good impression upon·the guests.

When Sitting Bull was called upon, the soldier motioned to him and he rose clumsily, but to the astonishment and horror of the soldier, said: "I hate you. I hate you. I hate all the white people. You are thieves and liars. You have taken away our land and made us outcasts, so I hate you." The soldier, sure there were very few in the audience with any knowledge of the language, realized it was up to him to preserve peace. He sat quietly until Sitting Bull had finished and then, probably with every hair on his head standing on end, he rose smiling and delivered, as the interpretation, the friendly, courteous speech he had prepared which met with approval of the crowd.

The year 1884 brought more innovations to the Sells Brothers Enormous Shows when they opened in Co-

lumbus, Ohio, on April 16. This was the first display of their 50-cage menagerie and also marked the first time Annie Oakley was billed in an outdoor show as a markswoman. Butler and Oakley appeared in the olio as "The Great Far West Rifle Shots" and also performed in a pantomime—Frank as Quaker Starchback and Annie as Mrs. Old One-Two.

For seven months in 1884, the Sells Brothers Circus crisscrossed the Middle West, dipping into Texas in October. By December 1, they reached New Orleans, where arrangements were made to entertain crowds expected at the Cotton Centenary fair marking the hundredth year

THE BIGGEST - THE GREATEST
THE VERY BEST
SELLS BROS.'
MAMMOTH 50 CAGE MENAGERY
And Great 4--Ring Circus !

Drawn by its Ponderous Locomotives. Its Great Trains are Coming, and the Big Show will exhibit at

Wausau
Until Tuesday JULY 15
IN ALL ITS MAGNIFICIENT PROPORTIONS.

OCEANS OF WEALTH INVESTED IN WORLDS OF WONDERS

The Vast and Limitless Dominians of Air Earth and Water, impoverished to complete this Gigantic

COLOSSAL AND ASTONISHING ENTIRETY !

An Authentic Convocation, consisting of representatives of the Human Family from every Land and Clime of Sun and Snow! Hundreds of Flying Steeds! Hundreds of Interpid Male and Female Artists! Thousandf of Huge Beasts! An Endless Array of Wonders! More Sights than Tongue Can Tell! More of the Curious, the Strange and the Wonderful, than has ever before or will ever again be witnessed.

Come to the Big Show ! Come to the Great Show !
COME TO THE ONLY GRAND SHOW.

The Only All-including Zoological Collection Ever Witnessed by man. Look for the wonder greater than all the rest,

THE CHILDREN OF EARTH AND OCEAN

The Greatest of All Amphibious Pachyderms. The Only Living Pair of Hippotami Ever Beheld Since the Dawn of Creation, as Captives by Master Man. These Huge Scriptural Behemoths Sweat Great Beads of Blood at Every Pore.

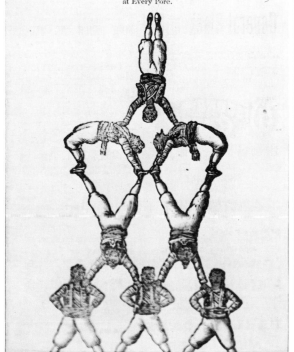

Emperor, The Giant Elephant
NABOR, the Coal Black Sacred Elephant.

THE ONLY LIVING FIVE-TON THREE-HORNED BLACK RHINOCEROS

Herds of Giraffes, Elands, Dromedaries, Camels and Zebras. Twelve teams of Elephant and Camels in Silk and Silver Harness. Drove of Kangaroos. Droves of Antelopes, Moose, Cape Buffaloes, trained Kentucky Thoroughbreds. A whole Cavalcade of Elephants. A drove of Lapland Reindeer, A World-Wide Collection. Dens of Arobian Sians, Polar Bears, Wild Tigers, Leopards, Jaguars, Hyenas. Lairs of Serpents, Crocodiles, Alligatros, Hosts of Heaven-Soaring Birds. Flocks of Ostriches. Whole clouds of Plumage. A Dazzling, Superb, Glowing Constellation of

200--ALL SUPERIOR STARS--200

Mr. Jas. Robinson,	**Miss Mildred Gardner**
The acknowledged by all Champion Bareback Rider.	Empress of the Side Sadler and Grand mistress of manege riders.
SENOR DON JERENIMO BELL	**MISS POLLIE LEE**
The Great Spanish Four and Six-Horse Rider.	The Only Living Lady Juggling Equestrienne.
M'lle Adelaide Cordona	**Miss MAGGIE CLAIRE**
The Interpid Lady Four-Horse Rider.	The Wonderful Flying Woman.

FRANK H. GARDNER, Master of the Horse, and Greatest LEAPING EQUESTRIAN ON EARTH.

THE BEAUTIFUL PURTIS FAMILY,	LESLIE BROTHERS,
MR. JOHN FURVIS.	BUTLER AND OAKLEY,
MR. JAMES STOW.	THE MARTINETTI FAMILY,
CORDELLO AND AUSTIN,	MR. WILLIAM SELLS.

And nearly 200 others, the whole forming an array of Circus Talent Superior to Any Ever Witnessed in the World.

Consisting of all the various ßons of man. Weird, Wild, Wonderful, Cannibalistic, Savage, Barbaric, Civilized and Semi-Civilized, from the Clans, Tribes and Nations of the World. Troupes of Triple Somersaultists, Double Somersaultists, Antipodeanists, French Voltigeurs, Athletes, Gymnasts, Contortionists, High Slack-Wire Walkers, High Tight-Rope Walkers, High Flying Trapezists, High Ring Flyers. Six Simultaneous Acts in Four Great Circus Rings, on an Elevated Stage and High in the Circumambient Air.

THE GREATEST SPECTACULAR STREET PAGEANT

Ever Beheld, Completely Overshadowing and Surpassing All Previously-attempted Displays of Pomp and Brilliancy. Hundreds of Prancing Horses, of Elephants and Camels gaviy caparisoned in Silk and Silver harness, hundreds of Golden Chariots, Blazing Vans, Gorgeous Crystal Cages and Brilliant Band Wagons, 1,000 Brave men, Fair Women and Rosy Children—the whole forming an Irreproachable Cavalcade, Scores of Dens of Living Wild Animals Open in the Streets.

1884

15

16. *"Butler and Oakley" in another Sells advertising piece, 1884.*

of cotton export. Unfortunately, rainy weather marred the celebration and, after eight performances, the long show train left for winter quarters at "Sellsville" outside Columbus, Ohio. They had traveled over 11,000 miles during the season.

While in New Orleans, the Butlers visited the grounds of a competing show, Buffalo Bill's Wild West. The publicity called it "America's National Entertainment—Led by the Famed Scout and Guide BUFFALO BILL (Hon. W. F. Cody) Artistically Blending Life-Like, Vivid and Thrilling PICTURES OF WESTERN LIFE."

Here, Frank and Annie were impressed by the care given the Indian ponies, buffalo and steers. In spite of the deluge of rain and the problems it created, the livestock rated special attention. The program featured wing shooting (flying targets) by world champion Captain A. H. Bogardus and his four sons, and shooting on horseback by Buffalo Bill.

Time obscures the next development in Annie's career. Did Butler ask to be hired as a team or did Cody come to them? Whichever way it was, they did join the Buffalo Bill's Wild West in April 1885 and Annie was prominently featured. Frank left the arena as a performer, but originated many of her back-bending and mirror shots, cared for her guns and always represented her in business affairs.

3

Early History of Buffalo Bill's Wild West

In 1882, when Butler and Oakley were busy playing local opera houses and traveling with the Sells Brothers Circus, a famous Nebraskan dreamed of an exhilarating outdoor entertainment. Little did Annie Oakley realize how her fame would spread after she joined this unique show.

William F. Cody, or "Buffalo Bill," as he was called, had a life style that caught the imagination of a country drifting into a mechanical age. Almost every American had some friend or relative who had "gone West," and often those who went West were not the greatest correspondents. Consequently, there was a great thirst on the part of those who had stayed at home to learn more about what went on out there in the new territories. Buffalo Bill was just the person to supply this need with his exciting Wild West spectacular.

17. A youthful William Frederick Cody. (Carte-de-visite photo by Napoleon Sarony, N.Y.; photocopy by Jack Richard)

The first outdoor show organized by Buffalo Bill was the "Old Glory Blow Out" held on July 4, 1882, in North Platte, Nebraska, to commemorate the founding of the United States. It was a typical frontier-day bash, with prizes offered for cowboy contests in riding and shooting—what we now consider a rodeo.

The next phase of Cody's showmanship lasted the single summer season of 1883. This show, "The Wild West, Hon. W. F. Cody and Dr. W. F. Carver's Rocky Mountain and Prairie Exhibition," was moderately successful, but ended in a division of the assets owing to a conflict between Cody and Carver. The program was typical of later shows, but the participants needed better direction than was shown during the 1883 season.

Opening May 17 in Omaha, Nebraska, the troupe moved on to Iowa, Illinois, Kentucky, Indiana, New York, Connecticut and Massachusetts. In July they were at the Prospect Fairgrounds in Brooklyn.

When they reached the Brighton Beach Race Track at Coney Island in August, it was decided to erect bleachers for the audience and perform there for five weeks. In a letter to his "mother-sister," Julia Cody Goodman, dated August 16, 1883, from Coney Island, Brother Will (Buffalo Bill) wrote:

> Have went to a big expense fitting up a place here—and as the watering season is about over it won't be worth much this year, but will be good for next. I am not much ahead on the summer in cash, but I have my show all clear, and a fine place built here. I have over a hundred head of stock—ten head of fine race horses, the finest six mule coach train in the world and seventy head of good saddle horses—and the foundation laid for a fortune before long. The papers say I am the coming Barnum. [Quoted by permission of Stella Adelyn Foote, *Letters from Buffalo Bill*]

In a letter from Youngstown, Ohio, dated September 24, 1883, Brother Will mentioned that he wanted to divorce his wife of 17 years, Louisa Frederici Cody—perhaps the first written reference to this intention. He complained that she was trying to ruin him financially and "bust up" his horse ranch in Nebraska. This was the 4,000-acre Scout's Rest Ranch near North Platte. (There were no divorce proceedings until 1905.)

In the same letter he explained he hadn't made much money because the advertising bills for such a relatively new show had been high, but thought next year he

would clear a fortune with it. The season ended in Omaha, Nebraska, in October.

In 1884 Cody formed a new partnership with Nate Salsbury, whom he had met in New York about two years earlier. This agreement between the two men marked the beginning of a mutually advantageous relationship that lasted for 19 years. Salsbury, author and comedian, continued to tour with his very popular company, Salsbury's Troubadours, during the 1884 season. Meanwhile "Buffalo Bill's Wild West—America's National Entertainment," with many of the same personnel as in the 1883 season, opened in May 1884 in St. Louis, Missouri, and continued east by way of Chicago through the New England states to Canada. Bad weather plagued them even after they opened at the above-mentioned Cotton Centenary Exposition in New Orleans during Christmas week. While camped in a field beyond Audubon Park, they endured 44 straight days of rain.

The circus Hall of Fame in Sarasota, Florida, displays an 1884 program book that tells about various members of the group:

> *Captain A. H. Bogardus*, the distinguished exponent of marksmanship, has been singularly blessed in his domestic relations and is the proud father of a large family—three daughters and four sons.
>
> The eldest, *Eugene*, 19, became so early imbued with a love for his father's profession that when 11 he was quite an expert in the field, having the practical experience that association with such an adept tutor could alone give. When the father went to England in 1878, young Eugene accompanied him and shot his first match with a gentleman at Woolwich Gardens, London. He won the "Boy's Champion Medal" with his .44 Winchester. While over there, his father bought a William and C. Scott shotgun in Birmingham.

18. *Louisa Cody, wife of Buffalo Bill.* 19. *Scout's Rest Ranch, Cody's home near North Platte, Nebraska.*

18

19

20

20. *Buffalo Bill's street parade near Union Square, preceding his show's New York City performance in September 1884. Cody is on the white horse; the man with top hat in the foreground is Nate Salsbury. 21.Buffalo Bill's Wild West troupe in Philadelphia, 1884. Next to Cody is Adam Bogardus, surrounded by his four marksman sons. (Photo by William Phillippi & Brothers)*

21

Edward Bogardus, 13 years of age, has been behind the gun for the last 3 years, is a good shot with his rifle and is very successful as a wing shot after quail surprised in the field.

Peter Bogardus, 11 years old, commenced shooting at the age of 8.

Henry Bogardus, 9 years old, started with his father in Cole's Circus, shooting with a .32 caliber rifle, glass balls from the Captain's fingers.

Con T. Groner, the cowboy sheriff of the Platte (Lincoln County, Nebraska), was noted for capturing part of Doc Middleton's gang and foiling their plan to join up with Jesse James and rob a Union Pacific train. Groner was born in Columbiana County, Ohio, and when sixteen joined Co. D, 72nd Ohio Regiment, under Col. R. P. Buckland, and while at the front during the Civil War went through 13 battles. He was wounded at Shiloh.

"Seth" Hathaway, who rides the pony express, has passed years upon the prairies, preferring the vicissitudes and dangers of the rover of the plains to the luxurious surroundings that his family connections, their wishes and his future prospects would assure him.

"Buck" Taylor (William Levi), a man whose great strength, nerve, endurance and skill are historical in the West [Taylor was six foot five].

Jim Lawson, equally distinguished as a lassoist and roper.

Bud Ayers and *Dick Bean*, who will appear in feats of horsemanship, riding bucking mustangs, roping cattle, throwing buffalo, etc., eclipsing in agility and danger the Spanish matadors of old.

John Nelson, called "Cha-sha-sha-na-po-ge-o," who by his generous honesty of character and energy, has gained fame and respect among whites and Indians. Being a thorough plainsman, years ago his standing as a train guide was most enviable, being sought for by all. He guided Brigham Young and the Mormons across the then "Great Desert" to their present location in Utah. He married Chief Lone Wolf's daughter of the Ogallala tribe and has six children whom he supports in comfort by hunting, being especially expert as a trapper of beaver and otter.

"Utah Frank" is Frank Wheelan.

"Bill Bullock," leader of the cowboys, is part Sioux.

"Fred Matthews" manipulates the ribbons of the Old Deadwood Coach and is equal to his old friend and compatriot "Hank Monk."

For sale on the grounds are the following books: "The Life of Buffalo Bill" and Capt. A. H. Bogardus' books, "Field, Cover and Trap Shooting" and "Record, Score and Instruction Book."

W. F. Cody uses rifles and arms manufactured by Winchester Firearms.

The lightning powder of the Laflin and Rand Powder Co. was used in Bogardus' champion matches.

Composed by John M. Burke, this program was printed in 1884 by the Calhoun Printing Co. of Hartford, Connecticut.

Burke, nicknamed "Arizona John," was press agent and troubleshooter for the Wild West from its inception. He was just one of the executives chosen by Cody and

22. *"Arizona John" Burke, Cody's loyal press agent.*

Salsbury who were not only capable but loyal, staying with the show for many years. Jule Keen was treasurer and business manager. Joe Hart, a great linguist, was a natural advance man at home and abroad. William Sweeney, cornetist, was the intrepid leader of the band who cued the acts for so many seasons. Each had his shortcomings, but each worked hard to keep the Wild West exciting and colorful.

Salsbury's original concept of the Wild West was an equestrian entertainment, and over the years he developed his idea by engaging outstanding horsemen from Europe and the Americas. Eventually other kinds of acts were admitted, of which Annie's was among the most outstanding.

4

Annie's First Years with Buffalo Bill

Closing a three-month stand in New Orleans on April 1, 1885, Buffalo Bill's Wild West worked north and by April 24–26 they were giving afternoon performances at the Louisville Baseball Park. A newspaper ad promised, "A visit West in three hours to see scenes that have cost thousands their lives to view."

The Bogardus family had departed, and taking their place were Annie Oakley and Johnnie Baker, the "Cowboy Kid." (Baker grew up with the group, progressing from performer to director of entertainment.) Annie, who was 25 but looked much younger, had gained experience and stage presence while performing under her husband's tutelage in vaudeville and with the Sells Brothers Circus.

Many years later, in her biographical notes, she told of the thrill she had felt when she was first presented to the Wild West company by Colonel Cody:

My husband and I were introduced as one of them— the first white woman to stand and travel with what society then might have thought impossible. Every head bowed. I felt something like a wild gooseberry sticking in my throat as the friendly, rough hands covered mine, one at a time, as they passed with a "How! Waste!" meaning a "all is good." A crowned queen was never treated by her courtiers with more reverence than I by those whole-souled Western boys.

At the beginning of each performance Annie rode into the arena during the grand entry, and then came her solo act. Her astute husband, Frank Butler, decided she would be the star, and would assist her by planning the action, lofting the targets and caring for her guns. In all business dealings, he became her manager. This splendid partnership was mutually advantageous.

Dexter Fellows, who joined Buffalo Bill's Wild West as a press agent in 1895 and remained with the show until his return from England in 1904, writes about Annie in his autobiography, *This Way to the Big Show* (by Fellows and Andrew A. Freeman), in terms that must surely have been equally true of her 1885 debut with the show:

She was a consummate actress, with a personality that made itself felt as soon as she entered the arena. Even before her name was on the lips of every man, woman and child in America and Europe, the sight of this frail girl among the rough plainsmen seldom failed to inspire enthusiastic plaudits. Her entrance was always a very pretty one. She never walked. She tripped in, bowing, waving, and wafting kisses. Her first few shots brought forth a few screams of fright from the women, but they were soon lost in round after round of applause. It was she who set the audience at ease and prepared it for the continuous crack of firearms which followed.

Proof that Salsbury and Cody had the formula for an exciting and appealing show is indicated by the record-breaking crowds that attended during May of 1885 in Chicago. In scrapbooks at the Buffalo Bill Historical Center, Cody, Wyoming, are clippings that tell of the adulation received by Buffalo Bill and Annie Oakley.

In June the troupe was joined by another great attraction—Sitting Bull! In *The Life of Sitting Bull and*

23. Photo of Buffalo Bill inscribed to Annie Oakley. (Photo by Mocher) Overleaf: 24. Annie, holding a Stevens .22 rifle, as a markswoman for Buffalo Bill. She fashioned her own costumes, generally from washable tan cotton. 25. Annie with a colleague, Texas Ben.

20   *Annie's First Years with Buffalo Bill*

the *Indian War*, by W. Fletcher Johnson, Buffalo Bill is quoted as follows:

I do not know for certain whether I met Sitting Bull or not during the campaign of '76. He was not at that time a chief of any note; in fact, he was not much of a chief but more of a medicine man. It was General Sheridan who really made him a "big Indian." They had to have some name for that war, and I was on the mission at Red Cloud Agency when they were talking about what name to give it. They spoke of Chief Galla, Crazy Horse, and others, all bigger men than Sitting Bull, but finally decided to call it Sitting Bull's war, and that made him seem to be a great man, and his name became known all over the country. The first time I ever saw him to know him was when he joined my show at Buffalo, coming with eight or nine of his chosen people from Grand River. He appeared there before 10,000 people, and was hissed, so it was some time before I could talk to the crowd and secure their patience. The same thing occurred at almost every place. He never did more than appear on horseback at any performance and always refused to talk English, even if he could.

26. Johnnie Baker, the "Cowboy Kid," who joined Buffalo Bill in 1885 at the same time as Annie. This photo shows Johnnie as he looked in the 1890s. 27. A Johnnie Baker poster of the 1890s. 28. Sitting Bull and Buffalo Bill, 1885. (Photo by William Notman, Montreal)

At Philadelphia, a man asked him if he had no regret at killing Custer and so many whites. He replied: "I have answered to my people for the Indians slain in that fight. The chief that sent Custer must answer to his people." That is the only smart thing I ever heard him say. He was a peevish Indian, always saying something bad in council. He was an inveterate beggar. He sold autographs at a dollar apiece and during the four months he was with the show picked up a good deal of money.

The long show train took the members of the Wild West from Buffalo to stops in other towns in New York State and on to Boston. After a performance in Vermont there was a very successful tour of eastern Canada—Montreal, Ottawa, Kingston, Toronto, Hamilton and London. The show crossed at Windsor into Michigan, after the harvest, when crowds were best.

29. *In this 1885 group, Sitting Bull is seated next to an interpreter. Standing behind them are Crow Eagle, Buffalo Bill and the naturalist W. H. H. (Adirondack) Murray. Sitting on the floor is Johnnie Baker. (Photo by William Notman, Montreal)*

Late September found Colonel Cody entertaining the staff of Fort Hayes, including Colonel Offley, at the Columbus, Ohio, performance at the fairgrounds.

This first really successful season of the Wild West ended on October 11 at Sportman's Park in St. Louis, after playing to over a million people and racking up a profit of $100,000. By November, Buffalo Bill had returned to his pride and joy—Scout's Rest Ranch—until February of 1886, when he again headed up the Wild West.

Annie and her husband spent most of the winter in Ohio visiting her mother and enlivening the neighborhood with matches and shooting exhibitions.

The year 1886 brought an innovation to the Wild West routing. Instead of staying one or two days in each town, they were booked into Erastina, a resort on Staten Island, New York, where 20,000 people could watch the two daily performances. The show opened in June.

Prior to this, a shakedown tour had opened at St. Louis in May. They showed in Indiana, Ohio, West Virginia and Maryland before a week's stay in Washington, D.C., ending on Memorial Day.

At Erastina, frequent ferries brought eager spectators to the 12:30 and 7 P.M. performances, the latter given under artificial light.

There were newcomers to the staff of entertainers, among them a Civil War veteran known for making patriotic speeches and flag-waving, Sergeant Gilbert H. Bates; there were the cowgirls who rode in a horse race, Georgia Duffy of Wyoming and Della Farrel of Colorado;

Lillian Smith, a 15-year-old Californian, was a trick rider and markswoman who appeared with the Wild West for two years. She shot glass balls that were swinging around a pole on strings, and it was claimed she could hit a plate 30 times in 15 seconds.

Buffalo Bill entertained 1,500 newsboys and bootblacks at an afternoon performance at Erastina one July day in 1886. Ed Goodman, a nephew of his, and Johnnie Baker, the "Cowboy Kid," both teenagers, helped distribute a sack lunch to each of the boys. The audience was probably one of the most enthusiastic ever to view the show.

Buffalo Bill's sister Julia and her husband Al Goodman were then managing Scout's Rest Ranch, and during the 1886 season, Brother Will often wrote them about specifications he wanted included in the new home that was being built there. First, he wanted a three-room suite—a parlor, a bedroom and a bath. Next, he suggested ten-foot porches. In one letter quoted in Stella Foote's book *Letters from Buffalo Bill*, the following request was made:

> I want a side board in the house someplace, probably just as well in my bedroom upstairs, with some nice decanters and glasses. I don't propose to make a barroom out of your home, but must have a side board. All we big dogs have a side board so put it up in my bedroom—then if anyone gets full I can put them to bed.

This letter was written from Staten Island on Sep-

30. *Cody and Indian chiefs during the 1886 Staten Island season. Left to right: Long Wolf, Flies Above, Rocky Bear, American Horse (Sioux chiefs); Cody; Young Chief, Knife Chief, Eagle Chief, Brave Chief (Pawnees). (Photo by Anderson, N.Y.)*

tember 16, 1886. The following month he was able to go see his beloved ranch for himself.

After closing on Staten Island on September 30, the Wild West had a two-month rest before opening their first winter season in Madison Square Garden. Steele MacKaye had been hired to stage a "Drama of Civilization—a Spectacle of Western Life and History." Matt Morgan, famous for his historical panoramas, painted the heroic backgrounds for the different scenes of the drama. Complete with a cyclone (activated by a huge blower), the winning of the West unfolded before the eyes of the New York audience.

At first the Garden was filled, even the $12 boxes, and people were turned away, but by the middle of December, Ed Goodman wrote his mother Julia: "The show is not paying too well but do not know what it will do as the show business is all a lottery anyway." Possibly because they had been stabled underground at the Garden, the buffalo developed "Neumonia" and 16 of them died. The spelling is Ed's.

In 1887, the Golden Jubilee of a tiny little lady brought even more adulation to the enlarged Wild West show

31. *Sioux warriors playing poker at the 1886 Staten Island encampment. (Photo by Sarony, N.Y.)*
32. *One of the Wild West acts: an Indian attack on a settler's cabin; Buffalo Bill and a band of cowboys, scouts and frontiersmen came to the rescue.*

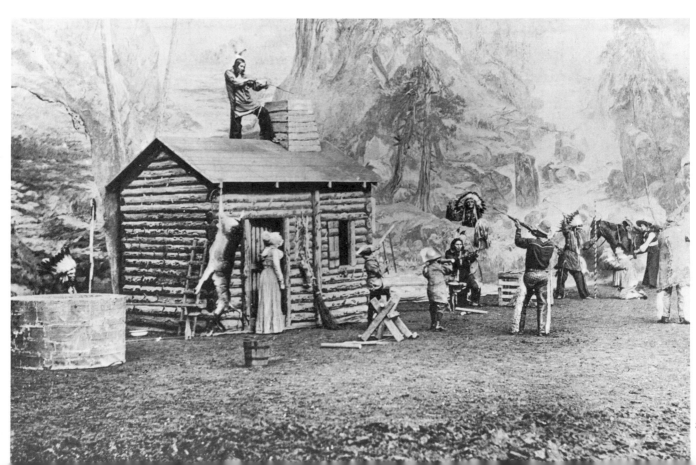

when the whole troupe appeared as part of the American Exhibition in London. Intrigued by the Prince of Wales's report, Queen Victoria sent a "command" that on May 12 she would view the Wild West for just one hour. She was so fascinated by this unusual show she stayed much longer. Later, when Buffalo Bill presented Annie Oakley, the Queen said, "You are a very, very clever little girl." The other markswoman, young Lillian Smith, and several Indians were also presented. "Red Shirt," billed as chief of the Sioux nation (he filled the void left by Sitting Bull's return home), was also presented to Queen Victoria. Through an interpreter he said, "It gladdens my heart to hear words of welcome."

When Buffalo Bill wrote the book *Story of the Wild West and Camp-Fire Chats*, published in 1888, he mentioned Lillian Smith but deleted any mention of Annie Oakley. One small illustration, however, shows Lillian Smith on one side of a reenactment of the Attack on the Deadwood Coach and Annie on the other side, each with a gun. Of Queen Victoria, Cody said, "A kindly little lady,

33. *Lillian Smith, a markswoman with Buffalo Bill's Wild West from 1886 to 1888. 34. Ed Goodman, son of Cody's sister Julia, and Johnnie Baker, about 1887. (Photo by Harrington & Company, London)*

35

37

35. *The Wild West troupe aboard the* STATE OF NEBRASKA *en route for England, 1887. (Photo by Merritt & Von Wagner, Washington, D.C.)* 36. *The company on the exhibition grounds in London, 1887.* 37. *Members of Cody's staff in front of his tent at the American Exhibition, Earl's Court, London. Press agent John Burke is seated in the center, with treasurer Jule Keen to the right of him; Salsbury has the top hat and cane. (Photo by Elliott & Fry, London)*

36

Annie's First Years with Buffalo Bill 29

38

Indians in Mountains

40

38. *In another view of the London grounds, Annie Oakley is barely visible beside a post in the center of the picture. Cody, in broad hat, stands beneath the buffalo head on his tent.* 39. *Artificial mountains on the London grounds, with Annie and Indians. (Photo by Elliott & Fry, London)* 40. *A famous British photo of a much-bemedaled Annie. (Photo by Elliott & Fry, London)*

H.R.H. Princess of Wales

H.M. the Queen

H.R.H. Princess Beatrice, Battenberg

Countess of Dudley

Grand Duchess Serge of Russia

H.R.H. Princess of Saxe-Meiningen

H.R.H. Princess Mary Adelaide

Duchess of Leinster

Princess Louise

Queen of the Belgians

Distinguished Visitors to Buffalo Bill's Wild West, London, 1887.

41

41. *Distinguished visitors, female. (Photocopy by Jack Richard)* 42. *Distinguished visitors, male.*
(Photocopy by Steinmetz)

King of Sweden

King of the Belgians

King of Greece

H.R.H. Prince of Wales.

Gen'l Lord Wolseley.

W. E. Gladstone.

King of Saxony

King of Denmark

John Bright, M.P.

18

Distinguished Visitors to Buffalo Bill's Wild West, London, 1887

43. *The cover of a rare 1887 publication of which no whole copy is known.* 44. *Johnnie Baker in action. When he performed this trick, he usually got into position, then got up, removed a sizeable stone from the spot where his head had been, and then completed his shooting.*

not five feet in height, but every inch a gracious queen. I had the pleasure of presenting Miss Lillian Smith, the mechanism of whose Winchester repeater was explained to her Majesty, who takes a remarkable interest in firearms. Young California spoke up gracefully and like a little woman."

This omission of Annie's name was due to her having left the show after the last London performance in the fall of 1887, when the others went on to Manchester. There are many engraved invitations and news clippings in both her scrapbooks and Cody's that indicate how British society and the press lionized the pair. Perhaps a jealousy had developed.

A second command was sent to the Wild West by the Queen for a performance to be held for the royal guests who had come to England for her Jubilee. It was given on June 20, one day before the official ceremonies at Westminster. There were probably more crowned heads at this performance than at any other outdoor show before or since.

After reams of publicity about this command performance, the British flocked to the grounds to see the show and visit the intriguing tent and tepee city surrounding it. Two and a half million people came. Business was so good that Buffalo Bill wrote his brother-in-law in July, "If you see a good place where I can invest some money, I can send it for we have a few scads now—and am liable to have more" (quoted in *Letters from Buffalo Bill*).

All during the London engagement, Annie Oakley's tent was filled with flowers and gifts sent by her many admirers. She was 27, but because of her slight figure she appeared much younger. Her husband Frank stayed in the background and many did not know of their marriage, so, as often happens with famous women, Annie received numerous love letters. One young man was so smitten that when he found out she was married, he went to Africa. Many years later he emigrated to the States, bringing with him as trophies horns from game he had killed in Africa; these he presented to Annie and her husband.

Many gun clubs asked the famed Miss Oakley to give exhibitions of her shooting skill and to shoot in competitions. A fee was never mentioned, but the day after an exhibition a purse of around $200 was brought to her. This, in addition to her Wild West salary, enabled her to

Annie's First Years with Buffalo Bill 35

PROGRAMME

of

Miss Annie Oakley's

Private Performance

Before The Members and Their Friends

of The Union-Club Berlin

On Nowember 13. 1887

At Charlottenburg Rase Cours.

1. Exhibition of Rifle Shooting.
2. Shooting Clay Pigions for straight.
3. Pulling the trap herself.
4. Standing back to trap, turning and firing.
5. The snap shot hitting the pitgin close the trap.
6. Shooting double or from two traps sprung at sam tirms.
7. Picking gun from ground after trap is sprung.
8. Same shot double.
9. Starding 20 feet from the gun, runing and firing after the trap is sprung.
10. Holding gun with one hand throwing ball herself.
11. Throwing two balls herself, bracking both.
12. Throwing ball backwards, picking up gun, and breaking it.
13. Breaking two balls picking ap gun and breaking im.
14. Breaking six balls throwing in air in four seconds.
15. Breaking threeballs in air at the sam tirms.
16. Breaking five balls in five seconds first with rifle others with shot guns changing guns three times.
17. Shooting ath twelf lif pidgings 25 yards rise **20 bor gun.**

45. *The program of Annie's private exhibition at Charlottenburg in November 1887.*

indulge in some luxuries, such as having some really elegant gowns made for her many social engagements. The London designers copied *her* ideas for riding habits and brought the Western theme into their collections. This was a real honor for the Ohioan who had learned to sew at the Darke County poor farm.

Annie and Frank accepted the invitation of the Kaiser to come to Germany for a period following their departure from the Wild West. It was here that she performed before the members and friends of the Union-Club Berlin, at the Charlottenburg race course, on November 13, 1887.

She had commitments in France but did not fulfill them because of ill health. Instead the Butlers sailed for the United States, arriving before Christmas. They rented rooms in New York City, where Frank, always a clever manager, began arranging public appearances and interviews and scheduling matches for the coming spring.

On April 30, 1888, the Wild West closed a six-month stay in Manchester, England, where they had performed in a structure similar to Madison Square Garden. They returned to New York City on a chartered boat, the *Persian Monarch.*

5

With Pawnee Bill, and with Cody in Europe

By early 1888, Annie had recouped her strength and again accepted matches and requests for public appearances. While playing to packed houses under the tutelage of Tony Pastor in New York, Annie and Frank probably wondered how the Wild West was faring. There are letters indicating that Buffalo Bill would have liked to leave the arena at Manchester before May of 1888, but was under contract and could not do so. Nate Salsbury left England on January 10 to make arrangements for the coming summer engagement at Erastina, Staten Island.

In the spring, Annie received an offer to appear with a rival show, possibly the one organized by Charles M. Southwell. Accustomed to the beautifully trained horses of Buffalo Bill, the Butlers were appalled at the condition of the animals they saw. At the same time, "Pawnee Bill" (Gordon W. Lillie), who had been an esteemed interpreter for the Indians of Buffalo Bill's Wild West in the early years, organized a huge show that he planned to take to Belgium for a six-month stand at the Grand Exposition in Brussels. Owing to the death of Emperor William of Germany and the period of mourning that followed, the contract was canceled. Suddenly it became necessary to obtain bookings in the United States.

May 24, 1888, found Pawnee Bill's Frontier Exhibition in St. Joseph, Missouri, with 165 horses and mules, 85 Indians (Pawnees, Comanches, Kiowas, Kaws and Wichitas), 50 fearless riders and 30 trappers, hunters and scouts. That made a lot of mouths to feed and a huge railroad bill. After working their way east from Kansas City and Indianapolis, the show was stranded in Pittsburgh. Frank Butler read of the Lillie dilemma and persuaded the sponsors of the eastern show to pay the railroad debt and bring Pawnee Bill and his group to bolster their entourage. Butler knew of Lillie's capabilities from having worked with him during the 1886 tour of Buffalo Bill's Wild West.

The reorganized Pawnee Bill Frontier Exhibition opened July 2, 1888, at Gloucester Beach, New Jersey, with two performances daily. Featured were Annie Oakley, Pawnee Bill—billed as "White Chief of the Pawnees—young daredevil who performs miracles with a rope and six-shooter and rides like a fiend on a big black stallion"—and his wife May Lillie, "World's Cham-

46. *Buffalo Bill before leaving England in 1888. He has an all-leather outfit and his favorite Winchester Model 73.*

47

pion Woman Rifle Shot." Possibly because of poor contracts and bad weather, the show folded in Easton, Maryland, in October.

Buffalo Bill's Wild West returned from England and again opened on Memorial Day at Erastina, where they stayed until the end of August. A two-month tour to Philadelphia, Washington and Baltimore ended at the Richmond Exposition in Virginia. Finally, Colonel Cody was free to go to Scout's Rest Ranch in Nebraska. Here he had another barn built specifically to stable his European stock. The responsibility of keeping the show going

47. Gordon W. Lillie ("Pawnee Bill"). 48. May Lillie, wife of "Pawnee Bill," in later life.

for two years and seven months, involving two ocean voyages and many decisions, had taken its toll. He was ready for a rest!

Frank Butler was busy arranging interviews and matches for his wife after the end of her role with Pawnee Bill. Her guns were on display for three weeks at Bandle's Gun Store in Cincinnati.

48

51

49. *Nate Salsbury, vice-president and manager of Buffalo Bill's Wild West, in front of his tent at the Exposition Universelle in Paris, 1889.* 50. *Annie in a Parisian gown.* 51. *Annie shooting clay pigeons. Illustration from a French shooting publication.*

Annie Oakley's contracts, whether with the impresario Tony Pastor or with Colonel Cody, always allowed her to engage in public shooting matches while in their employ. This served a dual purpose. It gave her more local news coverage and she shared the gate receipts received by the gun club where the contest was held. Also, Frank Butler was employed as a representative of the Union Metallic Cartridge Company and as a salesman for the Remington Arms Company. It appears that, between them, they played all the angles.

One shooting match was to be against an English champion, the winner to be the one scoring best out of 50 birds. In an untypical move, Annie Oakley was adjusting a trap when it malfunctioned. The spring ripped loose and tore the flesh between the fingers on her left hand. In spite of the doctor's admonition not to use the hand until the stitches were removed and the wound healed, Annie went ahead with the match. Trying to maneuver for a difficult shot, she again opened the wound.

Frank called the match, which ended in a draw when the foreign champion also missed his eleventh bird.

The Philadelphia *Times* carried an account of Annie's successful match with the champion Miles Johnson on October 6, 1888, and she was quoted in the Canadian publication *Forest and Farm.*

In December 1888 Annie appeared in the play *Deadwood Dick, or The Sunbeam of the Sierras.* It was billed as "the greatest and most thrilling border drama ever produced." The alliteration in the ads sounds as if they were written by the dime-novel author Ned Buntline: "Bold Border Boys—Bad Bucking Broncos—and Masterless Mexican Mustangs." A street parade on December 22, 1888, included, besides the star Annie, the Deadwood stagecoach and two Indians, Deep Water and Hunted Bear. In spite of copious publicity releases, and the enthusiastic acting of cowboys Pony Bob, Wichita Jim, Mexican Frank and Cheyenne Charlie, the melodrama was not a hit and closed the last of January 1889.

Fortunately, Cody and Salsbury now wanted Annie to come back and star in their show during their forthcoming European tour. Past differences were forgotten and the triumvirate of Cody, Salsbury and Oakley were ready for a new venture.

Annie's flair and skill attracted crowds to the show, and the partners wanted her on the program. On the other hand, she now more than ever appreciated the quality of the Wild West and realized it was a great setting for her act. The show offered her publicity and prestige, and this she wanted.

On April 12, 1889, the whole company left New York for Le Havre on the *Persian Monarch*. Thus began the group's first long European tour. After landing, wagons, animals and all the accoutrements of the show were loaded in freight cars and taken to Paris for the Exposition. This major world's fair, which celebrated the hundredth anniversary of the French Revolution, is chiefly remembered for the unusual edifice built for the occasion, the Eiffel Tower.

The opening of Buffalo Bill's Wild West in Paris in May of 1889 was a gala affair. Couturiers were busy designing gowns for the grand show. A clipping describes some of these creations as follows:

> President Carnot's wife wore a grey faille, embroidered dress with a lace shoulder cape and a bonnet trimmed with poppies. Mme. Christine Nilsson [the great opera star] wore a costume of electric blue cloth and Mlle. de Miranda was attired in a splendid black lace gown.
>
> Mrs. G. C. Crawford's costume was a pretty bit of color, being of scarlet surah. Mrs. John Monroe wore a complete Eiffel costume, one of the Morin and Blossier's Exhibition fashions. The material was of pale green and black striped silk. The mantle was of bronze velvet; her capote was black lace, trimmed with a garland of yellow flowers.

An old Parisian was heard to say: "I have seen many first performances during the last couple of years in Paris, but never have I seen one at which there was such a splendidly representative gathering of all the city."

Buffalo Bill's Wild West remained at their headquarters, dubbed "Buffalodrum," and performed for the enthusiastic French audiences for seven months.

Annie was competing in a match at Lyons when she ran into trouble. Frank Butler had been careful to bring Schultze powder with him from the States when they left earlier in the year; however, six months later, the supply was now gone. Following directions on the can of French gunpowder almost resulted in disaster. Using a wet-weather load on a hot day caused this smokeless French powder to burst the gun barrel. Fortunately, Annie was not hurt. After this accident, shells were loaded every day just before the match, with a close watch on weather conditions. It is rumored that French officials denied a request to import English powder.

After losing the match in Lyons, the Butlers returned to Marseilles to find an unsigned letter and a box waiting for them from England. Some kind friend had shipped two dozen eggs packed in the favored Schultze powder. After that, Annie's scores improved.

Leaving France in December, the show sailed to Barcelona, where they experienced one of the worst months ever. Besides being economically depressed, the town was having an epidemic of smallpox and a virulent type of flu. Illness was rampant among the Wild West personnel, and five Indians, lacking immunity, died. Frank Richmond, the dynamic announcer of the show, was also stricken and died. An intuitive showman, he had been a key person at every performance. Frank Butler was disconsolate over the death of his friend, but found it necessary to take care of his wife Annie, who had also become ill. As soon as the quarantine was lifted, Salsbury booked passage for Naples, where they opened on January 26, 1890.

Then followed a more encouraging tour through Italy with stops in Rome, Florence, Bologna, Turin, Verona, Padua and Venice. Some of the Indians were pictured in a gondola and touted as "the first American Indians that have visited the Adriatic." While in Rome on February 20, press agent John Burke, who was Catholic, arranged for the whole company to go to the Vatican on the anniversary of the coronation of Pope Leo XIII.

Next they appeared at Innsbruck. While in Munich on the last of April, the show was visited by the Prince Regent of Bavaria and his daughters. He was Prince Joseph William Louis Luitpold, uncle of King Otto, who was confined in his palace of Fürstenried, and adjudged unable to reign. So impressed was the Prince Regent with Annie Oakley's prowess that he sent her the following message: "If convenient, His Majesty requests the honor of an audience with Fräulein Oakley at 10:30 this morning." The request was granted and he appeared promptly. After inspecting her guns in her tent, he asked if she would hit a tossed coin for him in the arena. While there, the Prince was endangered by a renegade horse, Dynamite, and Annie Oakley, ignoring protocol, tackled the ruler and managed to get him out of the horse's path. As a token of gratitude, he sent her a handsome gold bracelet bearing the crown and monogram of Luitpold with a diamond solitaire.

During the show's stand in Vienna, Annie Oakley gave an exhibition for the benefit of an orphanage and, as a thank-you gift, received from the grateful sponsor, Baroness Rothschild, a heavy gold link pin, each link encrusted with diamonds. In her diary, Annie wrote the following:

> I really felt sorry when I looked into the face of the Emperor of Austria. My husband and I were being shown through the palace one morning and the Emperor sat at a table stacked high with mail for his perusal, but somehow he asked that I be shown into his august presence. He arose with a smile and greeted me with a real handshake, but his face looked both tired and troubled. I then and there decided that being just plain little Annie Oakley, with ten minutes work once or twice a day, was good enough for me, for I had, or at least I thought I had, my freedom.

The American ambassador in Vienna at this time was President Grant's son Frederick Dent Grant, who entertained the Butlers at a luncheon. The attendance at the Wild West show had been sparse, and Annie said this was because of the free music in the streets.

52. *When the troupe saw the huge statue of Columbus at Barcelona, one of the Indians said, "It was a damned bad day for us when he discovered America." 53. Overleaf: The troupe in Rome, 1890. Buffalo Bill is at the left; Annie is toward the right in the first row of standing people; her husband, Frank Butler, is the last on the right of that row.*

53

54

55

54. *Buffalo Bill and colleagues in Venice, April 1890. (Photo by Salviati)* 55. *Shown here in an unknown arena, Annie is assisted in her famous mirror shot by her husband, who is holding the target.* 56. *Pictured on a small German matchbox are Annie Oakley and Buffalo Bill's resourceful advance man, Joe Hart.* 57. *Buck Taylor (last man standing on the right) while he was still with Buffalo Bill's Wild West. Also in this group around the famous Deadwood stagecoach are marksman Johnnie Baker and Buffalo Bill, with press agent John Burke looming up between them.*

56

With Pawnee Bill, and with Cody in Europe 47

58. *Viewing the hostile Indian camp near Pine Ridge, South Dakota, in January 1891 are Buffalo Bill, General Nelson A. Miles and two captains. (Signal Corps photo 111-SC-85680)*

After exhibiting at Prague, the show went on to a huge success in Germany, due in part to the careful planning of advance man Joe Hart. He booked the Wild West into Magdeburg, Braunschweig, Leipzig and Cologne. They exhibited for a month on the Kurfürstendamm in Berlin starting on July 23, 1890.

While in Germany, Annie and Frank saw many of the friends they had made during their prior visit in 1887, after leaving Buffalo Bill's employ. In her notes, Annie told of how the German military staff watched the loading and unloading of railway cars, the horses and gear, how they broke camp, and how many men it took for each task. The Germans were also particularly intrigued with the kitchens—food storage, preparation and serving—and made copious notes and diagrams. The tour ended on October 28, 1890 in Strassburg.

There was an old castle at Banfelt, Alsace, south of Strassburg, which Nate Salsbury leased as winter quarters for the Wild West. Rumors that the Indians were mistreated were refuted by the American consul, who visited the camp. When Cody returned to the States at the end of the season, he gave the Indians a chance to go home; some of them did, under the care of John Burke. Buck Taylor, a loyal and talented member of the Wild West from its inception, and billed as "King of the Cowboys," decided to leave the show at this time and returned home to organize his own group. He soon discovered, as others have, that to participate in a company and to manage one require different talents. The Butlers accepted invitations to visit friends and do some bird shooting in Great Britain during the winter months.

While in the States, Colonel Cody was asked to aid General Nelson A. Miles during a crisis at the Pine Ridge Reservation. Since Cody knew Sitting Bull well, he thought he could reason with him and help settle the differences between the Indians and the federal government. He was granted permission to take gifts to Sitting Bull and bring him back to headquarters for a conference. Dr. Frank Powell, who had traveled with the Wild West in 1885, accompanied Colonel Cody.

President Harrison, alerted by a telegram from Indian agent James McLaughlin, ordered Cody to turn back without contacting Sitting Bull. General Miles was severely criticized by his fellow officers in Washington for delegating such a job to a civilian.

On December 18, 1890, Sitting Bull was arrested by a contingent of Indian police but exactly what happened is not clear. One version relates he was taunted by a son and resisted at the last minute. Two of the ghost dancers fired on the police and, in the ensuing fracas, Sitting Bull was shot and killed.

After the travesty at Wounded Knee Creek on December 29, the fugitive Indians made camp. By January 16, 1891, all of the resisting Indians had surrendered and the services of "advisory scout" Cody were no longer needed.

6
Adventures in 1891 and 1892

Early in 1891, while the Butlers were in winter quarters with the show, Cody, relaxing at North Platte after the Sitting Bull episode, wrote them two letters that are now preserved at the Garst Museum in Greenville, Ohio. These letters reveal information on the Colonel's private life.

Handsome, easygoing Colonel Cody was always attractive to the many women he met during his long career as a showman. His puritanical wife Louisa so disliked his companions that she refused to entertain when they came to Scout's Rest Ranch in Nebraska. This, of course, led to dissension between the two and made Cody even more vulnerable to female attention.

In his letter of January 19, addressed to Annie, he refers to his activity on the war front at Pine Ridge, North Dakota. He also mentions an erroneous report of

59. *Viola Katherine Clemmons as she appeared in* A Lady of Venice *in 1894.*

her death in Buenos Aires, first published in French papers. The cryptic last line of the letter, "I hear V.C. is in N.Y.," may refer to his erstwhile friend and protégée Viola Katherine Clemmons, whom he had met when the Wild West first appeared in London in 1887.

In the second letter, dated January 27, from Cody to Butler, he acknowledges receipt of a registered packet containing letters from V.C. and requests: "if you have any more send them along. . . . She is to swift & dishonest for me — Those were all lies about her getting letters & cables from me. Would like to know what she done in London & . . . who was the favorite she smiled upon there."

Later, Cody changed his mind about Viola, as indicated by his playing "angel" to her stage aspirations. He is reported to have lost $50,000 backing her two unsuccessful attempts on the stage. In England, she toured with the play *Theodore* and in America she tried her luck in *A Lady of Venice*.

One Washington, D.C., news release reported a fight over the fair Viola Katherine between Cody and Fred May in Chamberlin's restaurant. Cody, who flattened May, is quoted as saying it was "just a difference of opinion between gentlemen."

The family knew of the incompatibility of Bill and Louisa Cody, and in a letter to his brother-in-law and farm manager, Al Goodman, Cody explained how he felt about his wife.

The George Hotel, Nottingham, England, August 25, '91.
Al, if Mrs. Cody has any grain or grass on her place to be cut, I wish you would have it done for her—if she ain't there just go over and do it for her. I often feel sorry for her. She is a strange woman but don't mind her— remember she is my wife—and let it go at that. If she gets cranky just laugh at it, she can't help it. [Quoted from *Letters from Buffalo Bill*]

By 1904 Cody decided he could no longer tolerate life with Louisa and filed for divorce. The trial finally took place in Cheyenne, Wyoming, in March 1905 with character witnesses testifying for both participants. One testimony stated that Mrs. Cody accused her husband of intimacies with different women, especially an Olive Clemons, who resided with him in Chicago during the 1893 World's Fair. Presumably, this was Viola Katherine Clemmons.

60

60. *Annie tailored this costume of Scottish plaid and trimmed the blouse with a lace collar; Glasgow, April 1892.* 61. *Annie rehearsing at Earl's Court, London, in 1892. (Photo by A. R. Dresser)*

Another possible rival of Mrs. Cody's was Bessie Isbell, a press agent for the Wild West after 1900. That Cody invited her to his Wyoming ranch is verifiable, but their relationship is a matter of conjecture.

In spite of depositions from Cody's sisters that he and Louisa had been separated in 1877, 1885, 1887 and 1901, and that the family had been instrumental in the 1877 reconciliation, Colonel Cody's case was dismissed on March 23, 1905. Since Cody was the loser, Judge Scott directed him to pay his wife's court costs.

Katherine Clemmons married into the Gould family of Wall Street fame when she accepted Howard Gould's proposal in 1898. Later, when trying to get a divorce, Gould accused Cody of "criminal and meretricious" relations with Katherine before their marriage. Dan Muller wrote that Cody threatened to sue Gould for money he had lost on Katherine's ill-fated stage career and refused a bribe to testify against her.

While Cody was in the States (late 1890 to early 1891), Salsbury was arranging the route for the coming season in western Europe, and engaging outstanding horsemen from Europe. Joe Hart was sent to Russia to hire Cossacks. By the end of 1892 the company included riders from France, Germany, England, Russia, Mexico and the Argentine, in addition to the American cowboys.

On April 1, 1891, Cody sailed from the States with a hundred Indians and on April 15 a new season started in Stuttgart, Germany. After touring towns on the Upper Rhine, the show appeared in Holland and Belgium and was in England by July. After a swing through the industrial area of England, the Cody forces reached Cardiff, Wales, for the week of September 20–27. They stayed six days each in Bristol, Brighton and Portsmouth, and closed in Croyden on October 31. The Wild West then appeared at the East End Exhibition Building in Glasgow, Scotland, from November 15, 1891, to April 15, 1892.

62. *One of Buffalo Bill's twelve Cossacks from the Caucasus.*

Many of the company were thus spending their third winter abroad, and probably envied Cody, who returned to the States to straighten out his many business ventures and perhaps to find a little sunshine.

Frank Butler later told of the many men in Europe who tried to ride the bucking broncos of the Wild West show, but failed. A prize of $100 was offered to anyone able to stay on the horse. Each aspirant would remove his eyeglass and hat before mounting, and sometimes there was quite a stack of each.

Continuing in Butler's own words, "We had a surprise in London, though. A young fellow, wearing a monocle, derby, stiff collar and carrying the indispensable cane, dropped in to ride. We trotted forth the wildest bronco we had. Our hearts went out to the young man and we had a mental picture of his immaculate appearance all deranged. He rode the animal hands down. He turned out to be a wealthy Australian ranch owner. He sent the $100 prize to a charity organization. Incidentally, he was the husband of Madame Melba, the opera singer."

Actually, Charles F. Armstrong, Nellie Melba's husband, was not an Australian, but was born in Britain, the youngest son of Sir Andrew Armstrong of Ireland. He met Nellie Mitchell when he was working in Australia, and they were married there in 1882. Later they went to Europe, where Melba studied and made her debut.

Leaving their Scottish winter quarters in April 1892, Cody, Salsbury and company again entertained crowds attending the Horticultural Exhibition at Earl's Court, London, the site of their 1887 Jubilee performances. On May 7, 1892, there was even a command performance before Queen Victoria in an improvised arena at Windsor Castle. This occasion lent itself to great publicity releases.

After visiting the Wild West encampment in London in 1892, the Western artist Frederic Remington wrote in the September 3 issue of *Harper's Weekly*: "Next year the whole outfit is coming over to the [Chicago] World's Fair with the rest of Europe, and they are going to bring specimens of all the continental cavalry. The Sioux will talk German, the cowboys already have an English accent and the 'guachos' [*sic*] will be dressed in good English form."

The show closed on October 12 and, after three and a half years abroad, the troupe boarded the ship *Mohawk* and arrived back in New York on October 26.

Cody went to his home in Nebraska and immediately began working on plans for the presentation of his Wild West at the great exposition in Chicago in 1893. The animals, rolling stock and gear were sent to winter quarters in Bridgeport, Connecticut.

Annie and her husband, tired of living out of trunks, decided to build a home on Grant Avenue in Nutley, New Jersey. Here they made friends and enjoyed the quiet atmosphere of the town but really didn't spend much time there.

7
From 1893 to 1898

After months of careful preparation, "Buffalo Bill's Wild West and Congress of Rough Riders of the World"—the new name of the show, featured on all of the posters after 1892—opened in a downpour at the World's Columbian Exposition in Chicago. The date was April 3, 1893, about a month before the fair opened. Salsbury, denied an area inside the grounds, had leased 14 acres very close to the 62nd Street entrance and the terminus of the el. Even though the grandstand seated 18,000, on many occasions spectators were turned away, so popular was the show. Not one performance was canceled during the 186-day season, making it one of the most successful in outdoor-show history. Never before had so many people been intrigued by the savage charm of the Wild West as portrayed by Cody, Salsbury and company. The magnificent riding, roping and showmanship of the Congress of Rough Riders of the World was an extra bonus, a whole new segment, long planned and finally perfected for the Chicago crowds. Many foreign visitors came to the World's Columbian Exposition as much to see Chicago and the Middle West as to view the fair. They particularly appreciated the attention paid in the show to the British Lancers, the Cossacks, the French Chasseurs and the German Uhlans, each smartly dressed in a unique uniform. The American cowboys, the South American gauchos and the Arabs were more casually dressed in native attire.

Annie Oakley, who always appeared first on the program just after the Grand Review, had 35 different costumes fashioned for the long Chicago summer. She enjoyed being on location for the season, which made it much easier to care for guns and wardrobe. Her brightly carpeted tent was a rendezvous for the children of the company and headquarters for visiting friends. No queen received more admirers in court that summer than did little "Missie," as Buffalo Bill called her.

Through shrewd management, the Wild West partners were able to clear nearly a million dollars profit from their 1893 exhibition in Chicago, a record income that was far greater than the following season's.

The year 1894 brought several innovations to Annie Oakley's career and consequently new audiences. The first occasion was her appearance at the Nutley, New

63. *An Annie Oakley poster (by the Enquirer Company of Cincinnati) bearing the full new name of the show.*

65

64. *A poster by A. Hoen & Co., Baltimore.* 65. *Another poster of the same period showing Annie's prowess in the arena.*

Jersey, Amateur Circus in March. Of course, she was not an amateur, but participated for the fun of it and to help her neighbors raise money for their favorite charity. Trains brought crowds right to the arena.

Next was the recording of her dexterity with guns before the infant movie camera in West Orange, New Jersey, in early May. What an array of artists Edison hired to perform for the Kinetoscope! In 1893, two years after applying for a patent on his movie camera (the Kinetograph) and the corresponding peep-show viewer (the Kinetoscope), Edison built the first movie studio. The black tar-paper building was mounted on a swivel mechanism, making it possible to revolve the whole structure to catch the strongest rays of the sun when filming. The first subjects filmed were company em-

ployees. Pictures of Fred Ott's sneeze are famous, but the one taken of male technicians dancing together is more rare.

On May 4, 1894, Annie Oakley performed before the primitive camera some of the shooting feats that had made her famous. The first scene showed her firing 25 shots in 27 seconds with her Model 91 .22-caliber Marlin rifle; in another scene she was shooting at composition balls tossed into the air. Also photographed on the same day were Buffalo Bill and some of the Sioux braves from the Wild West. From the cast of *A Gaiety Girl*, then playing at Daly's Theatre in New York, were Darina Moore, Grace Charlotte and Florence Lloyd. Also appearing were Maggie Crossland, Lucy Murray and Mae Lucas, fancy-dance artists.

Viewed in the Kinetoscope, each film ran only 80 seconds and cost one nickel to see. Often a store was lined with Kinetoscopes, each with a different film to tantalize the eager public. An old Edison film catalog offered

66

66. *During the World's Columbian Exposition of 1893 in Chicago, Annie was honored by Governor William McKinley of Ohio.* 67. *This unique trunk was an asset to Annie during her many tours. It was just long enough to take her short costumes without folding, and because of its dresser-type top it served well in either a tent or a stateroom.*

Professor Batty and his famous trained bears; Dolorita; "the passion dancer"; the Englehart sisters, broadsword performers; and Layman, the man of 1,000 faces.

Buffalo Bill's Wild West opened at Ambrose Park, Brooklyn, New York, on May 12, 1894. The owners built a costly covered grandstand seating 20,000 and the grounds were conveniently located adjacent to the 39th Street ferry, but still the crowds didn't come. With a daily expense of $4,000, Buffalo Bill was frantic. The season at the World's Columbian Exposition in Chicago had been highly successful in spite of the 1893 panic, but by 1894 many people were in a financial bind and not paying for enter-

tainment—not even the renowned Wild West. This was the last year the show ever remained in one location for a whole season. The final performance was on October 6.

After her five-month engagement with the show, Annie Oakley sailed for London with her husband Frank, a horse (Gypsy) and 12 of Colonel A. B. Whitlock's foxhounds. The hounds, fresh from Bullittsville, Kentucky, were to be used in her new play *Miss Rora*, written for her by Ullie Akerstrom. The following review appeared in the *Hereford Times* of December 28, 1894:

> The play in which Miss Oakley makes her debut to a Hereford audience, is a four act comedy drama, entitled "Miss Rora;" her abilities as a shot are well known the world over, and during the first act she does some wonderful shooting, while in the last act, she shows herself to be a superb HORSEWOMAN.... She is also a LITHE-SOME ACTRESS and sustains the part of Rora with much vivacity, seeming to be completely enthralled with her part.

68

68. *A stirring moment in any performance of the Wild West was Buffalo Bill's entry into the arena;
here he rides his horse Duke. (Montgomery Ward Ethnological Series stereograph; photocopy by
Dolfinger) 69. Another thrilling act was the "Attack on the Deadwood Mail-Coach by Indians,
repulse of the Indians, and rescue of the stage, passengers and mail, by 'Buffalo Bill' and his
attendant Cowboys." Often, important persons at the show were asked to ride inside the coach.
(Photo by Goldie Brothers, Cardiff)*

Cow Boys;
Buf

70. *William Sweeney and his Cowboy Band,
photographed in Chicago in 1893.*

R. B. Caverly, her booking agent in England, expressed regret, at the end of the tour in March 1895, that her reengagement with Buffalo Bill prevented her from remaining longer, as he had turned down many offers for appearances.

There were two chief factors involved in a change of Wild West routine following the 1894 season. One was the failure of the summer stay at Ambrose Park arena to make a satisfactory profit; the other was the new manager, James A. Bailey. Nate Salsbury felt he was unable to continue as business manager, so he brought in Bailey, who was to provide rolling stock, animals and local expenses for a share of the profits. Bailey had run away with a circus as a boy, and circuses were his whole life. Under his management the Wild West took to the road as a regular day-stand show. After an appearance at Madison Square Garden, the season opened at Philadelphia on April 22, 1895. Then followed a 190-day stint of 321 performances. The personnel consisted of 700 people: performers, blacksmiths, canvasmen, electricians, musicians, cooks, sailmakers, watchmen, porters and candy butchers. The 52 railroad cars needed to transport the gear, animals and people traveled over 9,000 miles that year.

71. Cody with Mr. and Mrs. Nate Salsbury and their baby. 72. Edison's 1893 studio (the "Black Maria") at West Orange, New Jersey. 73. Annie as she appeared with the Wild West show at Ambrose Park, Brooklyn, in 1894. It was unusual for her to wear her wedding ring in publicity pictures. (Photo by Stacy, N.Y.)

71

72

75

74. *Annie posed for her celebrated mirror shot.* 75. *The "Cavalry Maze" act—displaying the precision riding of the "Rough Riders of the World"—at Ambrose Park in 1894.* 76. *Buffalo herd in Ambrose Park, 1894.*

76

In 1896 Buffalo Bill stayed at the Hoffman House in New York City while rehearsing the Wild West for its four-week stand at Madison Square Garden from mid-March to mid-April.

Excerpts from the diary of M. B. Bailey, who was in charge of the electric lighting, tell of the memorably bad weather the show encountered during its 10,787-mile trek across the United States that season. A month before the last performance in Moberly, Missouri, he recorded 162 days out, 52 rainy days, 19 threatening days, 18 cloudy days, 71 clear days. Three shows were missed because of bad weather and two because of a train wreck (Rudolph, Wisconsin, September 4, 1896). There were no Sunday shows.

Mr. Bailey reported two deaths in the camp. During the week stand in Chicago in early June, Salem Nasser, Arabian strong man, was hospitalized with typhoid fever and died. While the show was in Milwaukee in August, Edward Fletcher had the reins of a bandwagon switched from his hands and, in trying to recover them, fell to the pavement and fractured his skull.

Mr. Bailey did record some happy events in his diary. Like the time Annie Oakley's family drove 30 miles in a buggy to see her for the first time as a star. This was at Piqua, Ohio, on July 4, 1896. Arriving in Quaker dress were Annie's 61-year-old mother, her sisters and her brother John Moses. It was he who had probably taught her to shoot when they were children. Annie's nieces and nephews particularly enjoyed seeing the ammunition wagon where the shells were loaded before each show. Only the markswoman Annie and the marksmen Cody, Johnnie Baker and C. L. Daily used shot in their shells; the rest of the company used blanks.

On September 21, when the Illinois Central took the show to Sioux Falls, South Dakota, Annie got to see some of the plains for the first time in her life. The bandleader William Sweeney, Frank Butler, Annie and others decided to go hunting. Their bag was small but their spirits high. They returned with only one jackrabbit, one prairie chicken and a duck.

After three weeks in Iowa, Buffalo Bill had the pleasure of taking his great group to his beloved state of Nebraska. The officials of his hometown, North Platte, had long wanted him to give a performance there. Even though the population was less than 4,000, Cody directed the head canvasman to "stretch the full canvas." It's a good thing he did, because over 10,000 poured into the grounds from neighboring counties. The date was October 12, 1896.

On October 23, just before shipping back to winter quarters in Bridgeport, the Wild West appeared in Sedalia, Missouri, the home of 15,000 people and the railroad center of a prosperous agricultural area. At the time it was also the home of the pianist and composer Scott Joplin, who immortalized a popular local club with his famous "Maple Leaf Rag." Three years before, both Joplin and the Wild West had appeared in Chicago at the Columbian Exposition.

77. *The Indian attack on the emigrant train; Ambrose Park, 1894.*
78. *The Battle of the Little Big Horn, reenacted at Ambrose Park, 1894.*

After stopping to visit her mother in Ohio, Annie Oakley and her husband returned to their home in Nutley.

On March 15, 1897, Annie Oakley was interviewed at the Sportsmen's Show in New York when she talked on "Sports for Women."

During the year 1897 Buffalo Bill's Wild West traveled 6,108 miles and appeared in 104 cities in the United States and Canada. Posters heralded it as an "Ethnological, Anthropological and Etymological Congress—Greatest since Adam."

After a two-week stand in Brooklyn in April, the Wild West opened in Madison Square Garden on April 26 and stayed until May 15. Because of the attention being paid to the Cuban unrest, a new attraction was added, that of Captain Frank Thorp's Battery D, Fifth Regiment, U.S. Artillery. Daring drivers steered four galloping horses with gun and caisson over a difficult course.

After showing in New England, the troupe moved into Canada via the Central Vermont and Canadian Pacific Railroads. They stayed a month. This marked the first time they had appeared in Canada since the 1885 season, when Sitting Bull was part of the group.

They entered the United States at Buffalo on July 19, and toured New York and Pennsylvania before hitting Ohio right after a successful wheat harvest.

They were two weeks at the impressive new Chicago Coliseum, then on to a week in St. Louis, and south through Tennessee to Virginia, where they closed in Richmond on October 16.

As in previous years, Buffalo Bill's Wild West started the 1898 season with a grand parade in New York City on March 29. The show stayed at Madison Square Garden until April 23 and then went on to Brooklyn for a week.

After the American battleship *Maine* was destroyed in Havana harbor on February 15, 1898, President McKinley requested, and Congress voted in April, a declaration of war against Spain. Cody offered to join General Nelson A. Miles in Cuba, but through a combination of circumstances he never got there. Perhaps his responsibility to his partners, 467 employees and dependents, caused his delay in going to war. There is no doubt but that the Wild West would have suffered without his organizational ability. Peace was declared and Cuba became independent in December.

The train for the Wild West in 1898 consisted of eight sleeping coaches for employees, 15 stock cars for the animals and 16 flats for the electric-light plants, field pieces, prairie schooners, the Deadwood stagecoach, buggies and water tanks, and 35 baggage wagons for canvas, saddles and gear.

Annie Oakley and her husband had their own compartment in one of the coaches where they were able to brew tea over a spirit lamp and enjoy their privacy. There were no Sunday shows, so when they could, the Butlers found a hotel in the town they were to play on Monday, and had the pleasure of a larger room and restaurant meals.

During the months of May and June the show appeared in the east, going into the Midwest during July and August. Cody was flattered by the huge crowds that came to the Trans-Mississippi Exposition at Omaha, and

79. *A bandwagon of Buffalo Bill's Wild West in a street parade, about 1898.* 80. *Buffalo Bill's electric light plant, mounted on a wagon, in a street parade, about 1898. Built by General Electric in 1894, the plant supplied energy for lighting night performances.*

by the complimentary speeches made by Governor Holcomb and his old friend and employer, Alexander Majors. The latter said of Cody, "He stands not at the head of the showmen of the United States of America, but of the world." The show played to capacity crowds on August 30 and 31, 1898.

In his typical flowery manner, John Burke later wrote of this day: "Yet to him 'Cody Day' was infinitely and inexpressibly the most gloriously gratifying triumph of his memorable life, involving the highest compliment ever paid by any sovereign state, community or association to a private citizen."

Five days after the show in Cheyenne, Wyoming, a blizzard hit during the performance in Trinidad, Colorado on September 10.

October 15 marked their last stand—Charleston, West Virginia—and after the playing of "Home, Sweet Home" by the cowboy band, the train headed for winter quarters.

8

Last Years with Buffalo Bill

The 1899 Wild West parade in New York City heralded the beginning of one of Buffalo Bill's most successful seasons on the road. The first performance at Madison Square Garden, on the evening of March 29, was given before a packed house. Thirty-one performances were held at the Garden, including an afternoon exhibit which was free to orphans. Some evenings, the show was a sellout and the doors were closed early.

Next came Baltimore, Washington, Richmond and Roanoke. The last three weeks in May found the show in southern and central Ohio. After swinging back east in June and most of July, they returned to Ohio on July 24 (at Cleveland). The towns of Akron, Canton, Youngstown and Coshocton followed in quick succession. There was a week's stay in Chicago. In September the troupe visited Minnesota, the Dakotas, Iowa and Missouri. For six days they thrilled audiences in St. Louis, most of whom had seen the show before but still cheered:

> The two performances Sunday were attended by crowds which filled every seat of the comfortable and well shaded seats under the big canvas. Probably two-thirds of those present had seen the show before but still were agreed that it was bigger and more fascinating this season than in any previous year.
>
> First came the familiar but ever impressive grand review, and every detachment of the performers received an ovation on passing into the arena, the cheers for the Rough Riders and members of the regular infantry being the most enthusiastic. Cossacks, Mexicans, Arabs, Cubans and Puerto Ricans appeared successively in the long line, and after this had passed to the accompaniment of the Star Spangled Banner, played by the cowboy band, the regular performance began.
>
> Col. Cody made a brief introductory speech, after which Miss Annie Oakley, the celebrated shot, appeared and began her feat of breaking glass balls. Col. Cody helped her in throwing the small spheres, and her target shooting, which seemed to be equally true in aim whatever position she assumed and almost beyond belief in its accuracy. [*St. Louis Star*, Oct. 2, 1899]

In all probability, the reporter of this article was mistaken as to the identity of Miss Oakley's assistant.

James A. Bailey's influence in the show became noticeable by the appearance of typical circus sideshows on the lot. These had an additional admission charge over that of the Wild West. Bailey hired midgets, a snake charmer, a giant, a magician, a sword swallower and a group of South African Bantus.

Another innovation during the 1899 season was the inclusion in the program of a reenactment of the Battle of San Juan Hill. This introduced detachments from Roosevelt's Rough Riders, 24th Infantry, 9th and 10th Cavalry, Grimes' Battery, Garcia's Cuban Scouts, Pack Train, etc. The first scene was "A halt on the road to San Juan." The second scene, supposed to take place after a lapse of two hours, was "Storming of the Hill." Cody acted the part of Teddy Roosevelt and the Spaniards were represented by the Indians.

The 200-day season closed at Urbana, Ohio, with the 341st performance on October 14, 1899. In that season the show had covered 11,110 miles.

In 1900, after opening at Madison Square Garden in April, the Wild West followed the pattern established in previous years, first exhibiting in the East and then moving into the Midwest.

In April, Annie Oakley told a reporter from *Shooting and Fishing* about her guns. "As to my own collection of firearms, I have many shotguns, most of them hammerless. They weigh about six pounds. I use 12-gauge guns chiefly, because of the readiness with which I can procure ammunition for such gauge. I have, however, used with success the smaller gauges. With rifles I use the caliber best suited for my work. My exhibition work is chiefly with .32-caliber. With revolver I use the various calibers from .32 to .44. With pistol I use the .22-caliber."

July 25 found Buffalo Bill and his "Congress of Rough Riders of the World" entertaining in Annie's old hometown of Greenville, Ohio. As was the case with Cody's reception in his native North Platte, Nebraska, neighbors and friends of his female star were most enthusiastic.

On July 29 an accident in the railroad yards at Detroit resulted in the death of one of the cowboys. The Wild West show train backed down on a switch engine that was pushing several freight cars. The caboose telescoped into the next car, a sleeper, which was demolished. Later it was determined that the sleeping car was not built according to safety regulations.

81. *The Cowboy Band, about 1900.* 82. *An Enquirer (Cincinnati) poster of 1901.*

During the show's appearance in Minneapolis in August, Annie Oakley was interviewed by a representative of the *Minneapolis Times.* "Any woman who does not thoroughly enjoy tramping across the country on a clear frosty morning with a good gun and a pair of dogs, does not know how to enjoy life."

After the season was over, before returning to their home in Nutley, the Butlers visited in Ohio. Indicative of the abundance of game in that area is a news clipping from Annie's scrapbook: "Frank Butler, Charles Hahne and two friends from Greenville, were on a hunting trip recently in the North Star country [Ohio]. They were out two days and bagged 234 quail. Yes, Frank, we wish ·we could have been with you."

The eight-month 1901 season of the Wild West began with rehearsals in Bridgeport in March, followed by appearances in New York City. Then the three-unit train carried the show into the Great Lakes states.

The *Cleveland Plain Dealer* reported that on Monday, June 25, thousands of people were turned away when all of the tickets were sold early in the day. Disappointed spectators milled around the entrance; unable to get through the crowd, Miss Ruth Hanna, who had a ticket, was compelled to crawl under the tent. She finally found her seat.

A Pinkerton detective, J. T. Fallon, was retained by the Buffalo Bill staff to accompany the show and work with local authorities to prevent professional crooks from victimizing the spectators. Quoting from the *Delaware* [Ohio] *Semi-Weekly Gazette* for July 2, 1901: "The city police, reenforced by eight extra men and J. T. Fallon,

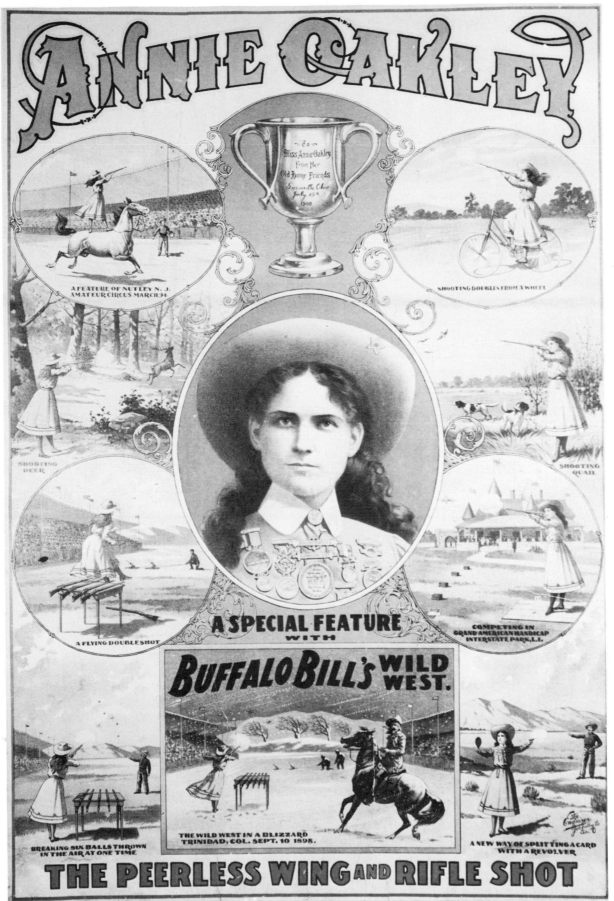

83

84

83. *U.S. cavalrymen on furlough were hired to reen-act the Battle of San Juan; 1901. (Photo by J. C. Hemment)* 84. *Annie with Gladys and Della, the daughters of Johnnie Baker, 1900. (Photo by Gray, Boston; photocopy by Oliver)* 85. *A formal portrait of Annie Oakley with her Remington Model 12 taken around the turn of the century.*

85

ANNIE OAKLEY IN THE WEST

THE GREAT CLIFF SCENE.
NANCE BARRY SAVES LIEUT. HAWLE

86

86. *Poster for Annie's tour in the play* THE WESTERN GIRL, *1902–1903.*
87. *Publicity photograph with a scene from* THE WESTERN GIRL. *(Photo by White, N.Y.)*

87

are deserving of credit for the able handling of the crowds which accompanied Buffalo Bill's Wild West Show Friday. Marshal Matthews and Mayor McClure went to Bucyrus and learned of the crooks and sneak thieves who were plying their trade there. Accordingly, when the crowd reached town, the officers were able to 'spot' the bad characters and keep a sharp watch over them. There were no robberies committed within the city during the show's stay." However, some men were arrested on suspicion, disturbing the peace and intoxication.

While the troupe was in Chicago from July 15 to 20, Amy Leslie, the well-known critic for the *Chicago Daily News*, wrote a glowing report of her old friends, as she did every time they came to town: "Always the foremost intention of Colonel Cody's incomparable show has been genuinely educational. . . . Annie Oakley and Johnnie Baker shot gloriously yesterday afternoon; and at night, in spite of a refreshing wind and gray fleecy clouds, both of these pastmasters in a brilliant field accomplishment immediately 'made good' without the slightest fuss or claim for other samples of weather or less hysterical women and children."

After visiting Iowa, Illinois, Kentucky, West Virginia and some of the southern states, the show was greeted by a large, enthusiastic crowd at Charlotte, North Carolina, on October 28. Following the evening performance, the Wild West company boarded the three-unit train for the trip to their last show of the season at Danville, Virginia.

The engineer of a southbound freight ordered a siding to let the show train pass, assumed there was only one unit, and when that passed, pulled back onto the main line. At 3:20 A.M. the southbound engineer and his crew saw the headlight of the show train's second section approaching in the night. Both crews jumped to safety just before the inevitable crash.

One railroader, sent by the Southern Railway to help clear the wreckage, said the engines seemed to have tried to devour each other. The mostly wooden cars broke into a lethal mass of splinters. Fortunately, there were no fatalities among the performers or crew, but 110 horses were killed outright or had to be shot. Two of Cody's personal mounts were killed, Old Pap and Old Eagle.

The third section of the train pulled onto a siding near Linwood, North Carolina, and was used as a temporary hospital. It was here that stocky Frank Butler carried his injured wife, Annie Oakley. At the time of the crash they were in their compartment in the second section, and Annie was thrown out of her bed against a trunk.

A news clipping dated October 29, 1901, tells of Annie receiving two slight injuries to her hand and back which were not regarded as serious at the time.

Annie's injuries were serious enough to require surgery and she remained hospitalized at St. Michael's Hospital in Newark, New Jersey, for several months. At the time no one thought she would perform again.

A terse news release announced the decision the Butlers made concerning their future plans:

ANNIE OAKLEY QUITS WILD WEST

Bill McCune, aide-de-camp of Colonel W. F. Cody, has a letter from Frank E. Butler, husband of Annie Oakley, the champion woman king shot of the world, from Nutley, New Jersey, informing him that he and his wife had resigned from the Wild West and would not be with the famous old show the coming season. Mr. and Mrs. Butler will take the road in the interests of a big cartridge factory. In concluding his letter, Mr. Butler said, "It is like giving up a fortune to leave the dear old Wild West, but a better position influenced us and we must go. Always your old friend, Frank."

As soon as she was able, Annie began appearing at scheduled matches. The second time she appeared after the train wreck was at Interstate Park, Queens, Long Island, on January 17, 1902. She tied for first place with Steve Van Allen when each of them made a clean score in a 25-bird event. They divided the purse and sold the gold watch they had won.

Annie told her friends that her hair had turned white within 17 hours after the accident the previous October. But in one of two news clippings found in Annie's scrapbook, Amy Leslie says of Annie: "Her hair turned white from being left in a hot bath at a health springs for forty minutes instead of one minute." One of the clippings in question had been mutilated where this reference is made, but is still readable. The other clipping must have escaped Annie's observation and survived intact. Who knows the true story? Why did 41-year-old Annie turn white suddenly? Was it from the scalding bath, or as a result of her injuries in the Wild West train accident?

In the fall, Annie began rehearsals for a play, *The Western Girl*, written especially for her by Langdon McCormick and including a cast of 16. McGiehan and Jepson, the managers, announced that the show would travel in a special car equipped to carry the horses, scenery and stagecoach.

After opening in Paterson, New Jersey, on November 6, 1902, the play went to Young's Pier in Atlantic City. Fortunately, Dr. Guion was in the audience on the night Annie's spirited horse turned too quickly and her face hit the scenery. He dressed the injury and the show went on.

The last performance of *The Western Girl* was in April 1903, after which the scenery was shipped to Darke County, Ohio, for storage. Annie's only appearance on stage after this was when she played in theatricals at the Carolina Hotel, Pinehurst, North Carolina, after 1915.

With the closing of the play *The Western Girl*, Annie packed her costumes but kept her guns oiled and ready for matches and exhibitions. In her scrapbook are clippings that refer to the Butlers' continued employment by the Union Metallic Cartridge Company and the Remington Arms Company. They were hired to give free shooting exhibitions using rifle, shotgun and revolver. Most of their programs were presented in the East and Middle West.

During the winter months the Butlers joined friends for the marvelous hunting near Leesburg, Florida. Often they stayed at the Lake View Hotel during the quail season, and entered matches at the Leesburg baseball

88. *Annie, with her niece Annie Fern Campbell (Mrs. Norman Swartwout), visiting Buffalo Bill at his showgrounds in 1907. (Stereograph by J. C. Hemment; photocopy by John Waldsmith)*

89. *Portly and gray, Buffalo Bill stands in front of a new ticket wagon at winter quarters in Bridgeport.*

ground given by the Florida Hunter and Fisherman's Club. The Leesburg band gave concerts at the hotel, followed by dances.

Buffalo Bill's Wild West had its first transcontinental tour without Annie Oakley's talent. The show visited 133 towns, in 27 states, in 201 days and covered 14,039 miles. In December 1902, the troupe sailed from New York for what turned out to be a four-season tour of Europe. Cody swapped territories and equipment with James A. Bailey, whose circus had toured Europe from 1897 to 1902. This was mutually advantageous.

Nate Salsbury, who had been in failing health since 1894, died on December 24, 1902, at his home near Long Branch, New Jersey.

The big three—Cody, Salsbury and Oakley—who had been associates almost continuously since 1885, were now forever separated.

9

Annie's Later Years

On April 3, 1903, a Chicago newspaper published an account of Annie Oakley being jailed for stealing a man's trousers so she could buy dope. Picked up by press associations, the story was published in numerous papers across the country. Two papers printed immediate retractions when it was discovered the woman in question was a "hophead" and an imposter. She said she was Anna Oakley, the daughter-in-law of Colonel Cody and widow of his son Sam. Cody's only son had died in 1876 at the age of six. The woman, whose real name was Maude Fontenella, later claimed she had been an understudy of Annie's.

In the December 1931 issue of *The American Press*, John W. Harrington wrote: "For quick-on-the-trigger action nothing ever passed the nation-wide barrage of libel suits fired by Annie Oakley, long champion marks-woman of the world. She winged newspapers big and little from Maine to Oregon and kept it up until her legal fingers went lame." Through her attorneys, Annie Oakley sued 46 newspapers and received favorable verdicts. Most of the suits were settled satisfactorily, many times for much less than had been asked.

Amy Leslie wired Annie immediately after the Chicago news release, and told her to sue William Randolph Hearst for at least $50,000 for printing the story in the *Chicago Examiner*. When that particular suit finally came to trial in October 1906, Judge Tuthill said that an attempt had been made to influence the jury. Annie received $27,500 from this one case, which was her largest settlement. Mr. Hearst was referred to in the news coverage of the proceedings as "Gloomy Bill."

90. *A Young Buffalo Wild West wagon.*

91

92

91. *Annie with the Young Buffalo Wild West in 1911. (Photo by Sherman, Newark, N.J.)* 92. *The Butlers and their dog Dave at Pinehurst, North Carolina.*

Later in 1903 Annie participated in the Grand American Handicap held at Blue River Park, Kansas City. This was the last time live birds were used in the matches. Also participating were Mrs. S. S. Johnston of Minneapolis and a vaudeville performer who went by the name of Wenoma. Wenoma was actually Lillian Smith, who had joined Buffalo Bill's Wild West in 1886 as a 15-year-old sharpshooter.

Annie's life was then fairly uneventful until 1911, when word came that Vernon C. Seavers wanted her to star in his own Young Buffalo Wild West show. The guns were packed and the Butlers were on their way. Seavers' show was much smaller than Buffalo Bill's, but it did have Indians, horses and lots of shooting.

Annie Oakley was 51, but still a great shot with a loyal following. Adults who had been taken to Buffalo Bill's Wild West by their parents now brought their own children to see her. Of course, this was before movie and television Westerns slaked the unquenchable thirst for Western lore.

Annie had been away from the outdoor arena for ten years, but the pattern was much the same and she again was headlined in the billing. Another shooter with the show was Captain A. H. Bogardus, who had toured with Buffalo Bill in 1884.

Featured besides Annie Oakley and Bogardus were the

Original 20 Ox Team, driven by Captain Stevens; Roy Thompson's Wonderful Horses; Bessini's Elephants; and the Rough Riders of All Nations.

The show appeared in many of the larger towns east of the Mississippi, competing with the 25 other circuses on tour in 1911. This was its first year to travel into Canada with its 21-car train consisting of two advance, six stock, seven flats and six passengers.

In 1912, this show combined with another and assumed the cumbersome title of Young Buffalo Wild West and Colonel Cummins Far East. Colonel Cummins was best known for bringing together groups of Indians from different tribes as an attraction at expositions. At the fair in Omaha in 1899, his Indian Congress included representatives from 31 tribes. At the Pan-American Exposition in Buffalo in 1901, he exhibited members of 42 different tribes, and 51 tribes were represented at the Louisiana Purchase Exposition in St. Louis in 1904. Besides Indians, Colonel Cummins brought to Vernon Seavers' show representatives of the Far and Near East: Burmese, Singhalese and Arabs, with appropriate animals such as camels and elephants. During 1912, something new was tried. While in Chicago for a two-week period in August, the show was held on a different lot every day, starting out at 38th and Wentworth on August 18.

At the end of the season, the Butlers went to a new home they had purchased on Hambrooks Bay at the mouth of the Choptank River near Cambridge, Maryland. Here they expected to retire.

In 1915, Annie Oakley and her husband joined the staff of the Carolina Hotel at Pinehurst, North Carolina.

94

93. *Annie with her custom-made Ithaca trap gun on the Pinehurst range.*
94. *A rare photo of Annie smiling; she is dressed for a Carolina Hotel costume ball.*

He was in charge of the skeet range and she instructed women in the use of firearms and gave exhibitions of her shooting skills. Even their dog Dave participated by performing his William Tell act (Annie shot an apple off his head). Thousands of persons came under the tutelage of this famous pair in the seven years that followed. Their summers were often spent at the Wentworth Hotel near Portsmouth, New Hampshire.

January 10, 1917 brought the sad news of the death of William F. Cody of uremic poisoning at the home of a sister in Denver, Colorado. Annie Oakley's tribute to him was published shortly afterward in the newspaper he had founded, the *Cody Enterprise*:

> He was the kindest, simplest, most loyal man I ever knew. He was the staunchest friend. He was in fact the personification of those sturdy and lovable qualities that really made the West, and they were the final criterion of

all men, East and West. Like all really great and gentle men he was not even a fighter by preference. His relations with everyone he came in contact with were the most cordial and trusting of any man I ever knew.

I traveled with him for seventeen years—there were thousands of men in the outfit during that time, Comanches, cowboys, Cossacks, Arabs, and every kind of person. And the whole time we were one great family loyal to him. His word was better than most contracts. Personally, I never had a contract with the show after I started. It would have been superfluous.

He called me "Missie," almost from the first, a name I have been known by to my intimate friends ever since. In those days we had no train of our own. No elaborate outfit, not even any shelters, except a few army tents to dress in. Among ourselves it was more like a clan than a show, or a business performance. Major North, one of the famous old pioneers, and Buffalo Bill, his two hundred friends and companions, a bunch of longhorns and buffalo, would come to town and show what life was like where they came from. That was all it was. That is what took—the essential truth and good spirit of the game made it the foremost educational performance ever given in the world.

Annie Oakley

95

95. *Another masquerade ball at the Carolina Hotel, this one held in February 1919.* 96. *Fred Stone with his daughter Dorothy (herself later a famous musical-comedy performer); she is wearing a Parisian dress brought to her by her father's partner Dave Montgomery.*

It may seem strange that after the wonderful success attained, he should have died a poor man. But it isn't a matter of any wonder to those who knew him and worked with him. The same qualities that insured success also insured his ultimate poverty. His generosity and kind-hearted attitude toward all comers, his sympathy and his broad understanding of human nature, made it the simplest thing possible to handle men, both in his show and throughout the whole world. But by the same token he was totally unable to resist any claim for assistance that came to him, or refuse any mortal in distress. His philosophy was that of the plains and the camp, more nearly Christian and charitable than we are used to finding in the sharp business world he was encountering for the first time. The pity of it was that not only could anyone that wanted a loan or a gift get it for the asking, but he never seemed to lose his trust in the nature of all men, and until his dying day he was the easiest mark above ground for every kind of sneak and goldbrick vendor that was mean enough to take advantage of him.

I never saw him in any situation that changed his natural attitude a scintilla. None could possibly tell the difference between his reception of a band of cowboys and the train of an emperor. Dinner at camp was the same informal, hearty, humorous, storytelling affair when we were alone, and when the Duchess of Holstein came visiting in all her glory. He was probably the guest of more people in diverse circumstances than any living man. But a tepee or a palace were all the same to him, and so were their inhabitants. He had hundreds of imitators but was quite inimitable.

His heart never left the great West. Whenever the day's work was done, he could always be found sitting alone watching the sinking sun, and at every opportunity he took the trail back to his old home. The sun setting over the mountain will pay its daily tribute to the resting place of the last of the great builders of the West, all of which you loved and part of which you were.

During the First World War, the Butlers' patriotism was shown by their entertaining troops and raising money for the Red Cross with the help of their dog Dave. In Annie's scrapbook are many letters of thanks they received from camp commanders.

Their friend Fred Stone enjoyed the sport of trapshooting during the summer months when his current show was closed. In 1922, when Annie Oakley and her husband were guests at the Stone home at Amityville, Long Island, Fred invited some of his baseball friends over for an afternoon. After showing his skill with the gun, he handed his automatic shotgun to Annie. Frank threw five targets into the air together and she promptly broke them all before they landed on the ground. One astounded spectator who hadn't recognized the now retired markswoman, asked: "My God, Fred, was that your mother?"

A miniature Wild West Show, held at the Mineola Race Track in 1922, garnered $11,000 for the benefit of the Occupational Therapy Society. Fred Stone, who planned the whole affair, led the parade with Annie Oakley, who later gave an exhibition of her shooting skill. In addition to the 50 or so horses, there was a fleet of flat-bed trucks, each equipped with a stage on which a performance was given by Fred's professional friends. Among the 4,000 spectators were many socialites, including the Vanderbilts, the Whitneys and the Hemingway boys. Fred Stone later wrote the following tribute to Annie:

> There was never a sweeter, gentler, more lovable woman than Annie Oakley. It was always amusing to watch people who were meeting her for the first time. They expected to see a big, masculine, blustering sort of person, and the tiny woman with the quiet voice took them by surprise.

While vacationing in Florida in November 1922, the Butlers were riding with friends when the chauffeur swerved to avoid a collision, and the car overturned. Annie was the only one injured. She was taken to Bowman Hospital in Daytona, where her hip was set and her badly sprained ankle was treated. The ligaments were so badly torn, she was forced to wear a brace on her right leg for the remainder of her life. Always plucky, Annie learned to overcome this handicap and again gave exhibitions. The Philadelphia baseball team was astonished when she demonstrated her skill before them while they were in Florida for winter training. At the Grand American trapshoot in Vandalia, Ohio, in 1925, her last public

97

98

97. *Garst House, Greenville, Ohio, built in 1852, was given by the Garst heirs to the Darke County Historical Society in 1946. It is famed for its Lowell Thomas and Annie Oakley Rooms.* 98. *A marker honoring Annie Oakley on the Anthony Wayne Parkway, Route 27, north of Greenville.*

appearance, she demonstrated her continuing ability.

By 1925, the Butlers had sold their home in Maryland. Annie was restless, ill and petulant. She thought she wanted to go home to Ohio to be among friends and relatives. First, she and Frank lived with her half-sister, Emily Brumbaugh Patterson, in Dayton. Next, Annie moved to Ansonia, Ohio, and was cared for by Bonnie Patterson Blakeley, a niece. By the late summer of 1926, Dr. Husted of Greenville felt his patient needed nursing care. Her sister Hulda helped make arrangements, and Annie's last move was to the Zemer and Broderick Home, 225 East Third Street, Greenville.

All her life Annie had been a modest person, and this feeling extended into her funeral preparations. She wanted a woman embalmer. Miss Louise Stocker, daughter of H. P. Stocker of Greenville, was called to the residence in October 1926. Calmly, Annie outlined her wishes.

On November 3, 1926, Annie died of pernicious anemia, and her funeral plans were followed in detail. Miss Stocker went to the home to pick up the dress Annie had designated. It was of apricot crepe de chine cut in a simple style. To find it, it was necessary to go through a trunk filled with tissue-wrapped presents, each marked with the receiver's name. Annie's white hair was parted in the center and combed back in a soft chignon. Because of the debilitating nature of her illness, Miss Stocker found it necessary to use makeup on Annie.

On November 4, at a private service at the home of Mr. and Mrs. Fred Grote in Greenville, close friends and relatives gathered to pay homage to tiny Annie. Her body was laid on a bed, since a casket was not going to be necessary. Frank Butler was so ill in Detroit that he could not attend the funeral. According to her request, Annie was cremated. The ashes were placed in a silver loving cup given to her by the people of France in 1889. This in turn was placed in a stout oak box and kept in the Stocker safe.

Frank died about three weeks later and his body was brought to Greenville for services on Thanksgiving Day, 1926. There are two markers on the grave sites of Annie Oakley and Frank E. Butler in the little cemetery at Brock, Ohio, but it is understood that the box containing her ashes was buried with Frank's casket.

10

Annie's Posthumous Fame

No one would be more surprised at the continuing popularity of biographical films and plays based on Annie Oakley's life than Bible-reading Annie herself. From the time she first assisted her husband in his act between scenes of a melodrama, she endured incredible hardships on the road. There were the difficult bookings (which Butler took care of himself), the drafty trains and the miserable boardinghouses. Later, when she was famous and her life was more glamorous, it is still doubtful she ever thought her life would be romantically portrayed on stage and screen.

She herself, as has been seen, appeared before the movie camera for Edison in 1894. Apparently none of this Kinetoscope film has survived. However, she can be seen riding in a Wild West parade as part of the film *Biography of the Motion Picture Camera*.

The first film version of her life, produced in 1935 and entitled *Annie Oakley*, is considered by some to be the most authentic. It was directed by George Stevens with Cliff Reid as associate producer. The stars were Barbara Stanwyck as Annie Oakley, Melvyn Douglas as Buffalo Bill, Preston Foster as Toby Walker, and Chief Thunderbird as Sitting Bull. Also appearing were Moroni Olsen, Pert Kelton and Andy Clyde.

In the 1940s, Herbert and Dorothy Fields conceived the idea of basing a musical on the life of Annie Oakley and expressed their thoughts to Richard Rodgers and Oscar Hammerstein 2nd. After encouragement from these knowledgeable friends, the Fields wrote the book of *Annie Get Your Gun* which Rodgers and Hammerstein produced. Irving Berlin, the composer-lyricist, returned to the Broadway scene after a four-year absence to write the 15 songs for the musical. The exciting sets were designed by theatrical genius Jo Mielziner, who had already completed 152 shows. The director was Joshua Logan.

Ethel Merman literally brought down the house when she opened *Annie Get Your Gun* at the Imperial Theatre, New York City, on May 16, 1946. Ray Middleton, appearing as Frank Butler, belted out his songs with enthusiasm equal to that of Miss Merman. Irving Berlin's bucolic songs fitted the book of Herbert and Dorothy Fields admirably, as proven by the continuing popularity of this typically American musical. A Winchester Model 92 lever-action that had belonged to Annie Oakley was used in the hundredth performance; it was loaned by Mrs. Spencer T. Olin of Alton, Illinois. The play ran three years on Broadway, with 1,159 performances.

Decca Records produced an original-cast album of six 78-rpm phonograph records with Ethel Merman, Ray Middleton and other members of the original cast, under the direction of Jay Blackton.

The national touring company of *Annie Get Your Gun*, starring Mary Martin, opened at the Texas State Fair in 1947. Fellow Texans gave the little Weatherford, Texas, gal a hearty welcome. The national company appeared in 49 cities. A revival of *Annie* was produced at Lincoln Center in 1966.

Paramount star Betty Hutton was loaned to Metro-Goldwyn-Mayer when Judy Garland became ill and couldn't appear in the film version of *Annie Get Your Gun*. The year was 1950. Billed as "The Biggest Musical Under the Sun in Technicolor," the picture was directed by George Sidney and produced by Arthur Freed. Besides Betty Hutton, those appearing were Howard Keel, Louis Calhern, J. Carroll Naish, Edward Arnold and Keenan Wynn. The musical numbers were staged by Robert Alton.

An original-cast album of the film was issued by MGM Records, with the MGM orchestra conducted by Adolph Deutsch. A few albums featuring Judy Garland were released and were considered rarities, but since then studio transcriptions of her performances have been made more widely available on records.

The Blue Book of Hollywood Musicals reports that MGM's version of *Annie Get Your Gun* grossed over $4,650,000 and realized additional income through TV showings.

By the time Mary Martin appeared in *Annie Get Your Gun* for television audiences on November 27, 1957, she had already toured the States with the national company. Quoting from her *Parade* interview on November 17, 1957:

> When we telecast *Annie Get Your Gun*, it's going to be as perfect as Dick and I can make it [Dick was her husband, Richard Halliday]. We've taken the show on the road. I've played it in front of live audiences. We've ironed out all of the kinks. We've done exactly what we did with *Peter Pan*—rehearsed, rehearsed, rehearsed. Why? Because on TV the public must be given our best. I can't disappoint the public and the critics. Giving love and joy to people—that's the driving force of my life.

99